ATLAS OF THE
ARAB WORLD

Contributors:

Compiled: M W Dempsey B A
Additional research: N S Barrett M A

Published by Facts on File Publications,
460 Park Avenue South, New York, NY 10016
© Nomad Publishers Limited 1983

Library of Congress Cataloging in Publication Data

Dempsey, Michael W.
  Atlas of the Arab World

  Includes Index.
  1. Arab Countries.   I. Barrett, Norman S.   II.   Title.
DS36.7.D45 1983   909'.0974927   83-1725
ISBN 0 87196-779-0

Color separations by RCS Graphics Ltd.
Printed in Italy by Poligrafici Editoriale
The Atlas of the Arab World
created and produced by
Nomad Publishers Ltd.

ATLAS OF THE
ARAB WORLD

Compiled by M W Dempsey B A

with an Introduction by John Bulloch
Diplomatic Correspondent of The Daily Telegraph
— specialist in Middle East and African Affairs

Facts On File Publications
460 Park Avenue South
New York, N.Y. 10016

Contents

Introduction

The Arab world today, that broad sweep of land stretching from Mauritania in the West to Oman in the East, from Tunisia on the shores of the Mediterranean down to Sudan with its frontiers in the heartland of Africa, is an area vital to the interests of the Western world. Not only is the Middle East the main supplier of oil to the West, it has also become a major financial power capable of influencing money markets in America and Japan, London and Paris. And because it is a confrontation area, an interface between the ideas of the two Super-Powers, it is a constant source of concern, a potential cause of crisis, a place where a local outbreak of hostilities could turn into a world conflagration.

In ancient times, it was in the Arab lands that philosophers and geographers placed the cradle of modern civilisation. The Garden of Eden was reputed to be in Mesopotamia, the land between the two great rivers of Iraq, the Tigris and the Euphrates. Sophisticated civilisations flourished on the banks of the Nile thousands of years before Christ, while Phoenician traders pioneered trade routes to far-off Britain and established colonies in Carthage. The long-lost Dilmun, a fabled land of milk and honey, was probably Bahrain in the year 4,000 B.C.

Then in comparitively modern times the Romans established their rule over much of Arabia, building great cities like Leptus Magna in Libya or the beautiful Baalbeck in Lebanon, where the fertile Bekaa Valley was known as the granary of the Empire. The Ottomans had their day, marking their sway with fine architecture copied from Constantinople, and a style of cooking which brilliantly used the available produce. The British and French had their brief moments, and left a tradition of learning and knowledge, understanding and tolerance.

But it was events long before which gave the Arab world its homogeneity and basic cohesiveness. For it was in the arid heartland of the Arabian peninsula in the seventh century A.D. that the third great religion of the world was born. The revelations granted to the Prophet Mohammed and the swift spread of the ideas and beliefs they generated were to become the one great common factor of all Arab countries. The need to take the message to the frontiers of the known world meant that at the same time the Arab language was spread far beyond what were then the boundaries of Arabia, and that Arab knowledge of the sciences could fertilise and mingle with the learning of the Western world.

That other huge event of long ago was to play its part, too, in shaping the Arab world of today. The Jews, conquered and subjugated, were dispersed from Palestine in a huge diaspora which was to take them to every corner of the world. Wherever they went, once a year, they made the solemn promise: Next year in Jerusalem. Now, they are back in that city holy to three faiths, and their presence there, the presence of the State of Israel in the Middle East, makes the whole area the flash-point of the world.

Now, Arab oil, Arab money, and the long-running conflict between the Arabs and the Israelis means that this crossroads of the world is of importance to everyone, no matter how far away a person may live. Yet it is still a little-known and much misunderstood religion. There is a tendency to regard the Arabs as a single stereotype, to think that all of them are rich, "oil Sheikhs", or wealthy playboys. The other standard idea is that the Arabs are poor, shepherds or simple peasants. Neither is right. Certainly the fellahin of Egypt, the farmers of the Nile delta, still till their land with oxen and dig tiny irrigation ditches to make sure that the precious water reaches every inch of their smallholdings. But these farmers watch television in the evening, the water they use on their land has been made possible by the High Dam at Aswan, one of the modern wonders of the world, and their sons have been tank drivers and gunners in the Egyptian Army.

In Saudi Arabia, the Western world's biggest supply and largest reserve of crude oil, there are rich oil Sheikhs. Many of them have been educated at Oxford or Yale, and far from wasting their money in the casinos of Europe, the majority will serve as civil servants, planning for the day the oil runs out and trying to ensure that their vast and empty country will not revert to poverty and obscurity when that day comes.

Outside the Middle East, people speak of the disunity of the Arab world, and wonder why the people of the 21 countries of the region cannot unite to become a new power bloc in the world. What is often not realised is that a Moroccan living in Casablanca is as different from a Yemeni in the Hadramaut as a Polish farmer is from a French writer. And both would have just as much difficulty in communicating with each other. Certainly unity is the dream of many Arabs, and is the declared aim of the ruling parties in Syria and Iraq. There have been many attempts in the past to bring different countries together, often with sad results. Syria and Egypt tried, Colonel Gaddafy in Libya wanted to unite with Egypt, with Tunisia, with anyone who would respond to his overtures. Now, Arab statesmen have learned the lesson that the wish is not father to the deed, that preparation is necessary; they have learned from the experience of Europe, both East and West.

Today, the United Arab Emirates in the Gulf are a proof that compromise and goodwill can make up for old rivalries and disruptive influences. In the Nile Valley, Egypt and Sudan are moving cautiously towards a form of integration, a natural outcome of their shared geography. In the Gulf again, Saudi Arabia, Qatar, Bahrain, the U.A.E., Kuwait and Oman have had great success in forming the Gulf Cooperation Council, an organisation which began as a common market and is now becoming a regional force.

Yet in every part of the Middle East, the Arab

countries and their peoples are subject to pressures which divide them and dissipate their energies. The war between Iraq and non-Arab Iran is not only a drain on the manpower of both countries, it also calls for vast expenditure by the Arab countries of the Gulf which back Iraq. Far to the West in the Maghreb, Algeria and Morocco quarrel over a swathe of the Sahara rich in minerals. And in the centre, Israel stubbornly holds onto the land the Palestinians say is theirs, while Egypt and the other States of the Arab League wrangle over how to solve the problems.

Nor are all the Arabs united in their adherence to the true faith revealed to the Prophet. The great schism over the true succession to the Prophet led to the establishment of the Sunni and Shia sects of Islam, which have too often been at odds. Later came other breakaway movements, the Alawites of Syria, the Druze of Lebanon. In Egypt and again in Lebanon, Christianity was never eradicated, so that the Copts of Egypt and the Maronites of Lebanon are powerful groups which at times have contributed to the troubles of the countries they inhabit.

Now, the Arab world is still in a state of transition. In a remarkably short space of time it has applied its huge oil wealth to provide industries and new cities, powerful armies and modern technology. Yet still it is not clear which direction the Arab countries will finally take, for the crisis with Israel means that much of their energies are diverted to that long struggle, and their long term aims seem bounded by the needs of what is a continuing conflict.

For many decades to come, the Arab world will remain a major supplier of oil to the rest of the world, a vast consumer of the industrialised countries' wares, and a powerful force in the economic sphere. Arab culture and ideas will have an impact on Western values, as they did when the Armies of Islam swept out of the peninsula to spread the word from the Atlantic seaboard to the khans of Central Asia.

For the student of politics or economics, comparative religion, history or the arts, a knowledge of the Arab world is essential. For the businessman seeking to win orders or to sell products, an understanding of the background of the area will enable him to deal more effectively with those with whom he comes in contact. And for the central reason that the future of the world may be decided by what happens in the Middle East, an awareness of the forces at work there should be part of every literate, thinking person's store of knowledge.

This atlas gives, in graphic form as well as in words, most of what needs to be known about the Middle East, the geography, the populations, trends, resources, manpower, military strengths and so on. It will be an invaluable help to anyone wishing to know more about one of the most vital areas of the world today.

John Bulloch

1 The Arab Nations

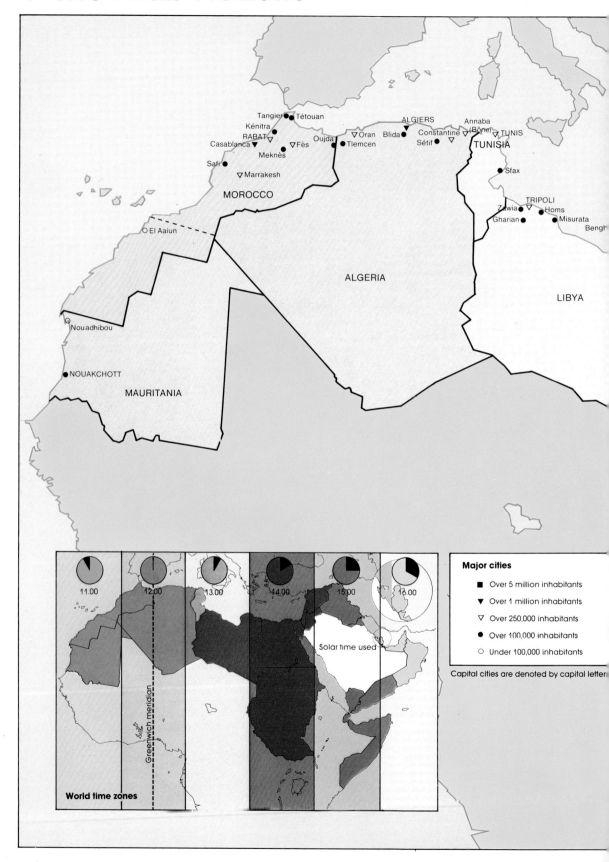

Tangier • Tétouan
Kénitra •
RABAT ▽
Casablanca ▼
Meknès •
Safi •
▽ Marrakesh
▽ Fès
Oujda •
Tlemcen •
▽ Oran
Blida •
ALGIERS
Constantine •
Sétif •
▽
Annaba (Bône)
▽ TUNIS
TUNISIA
Sfax •
TRIPOLI
Zawia • ▽
Gharian •
Homs •
Misurata •
Bengh

MOROCCO

O El Aaiun

ALGERIA

LIBYA

○ Nouadhibou

• NOUAKCHOTT

MAURITANIA

World time zones

11.00 12.00 13.00 14.00 15.00 16.00

Greenwich meridian

Solar time used

Major cities

■ Over 5 million inhabitants

▼ Over 1 million inhabitants

▽ Over 250,000 inhabitants

● Over 100,000 inhabitants

○ Under 100,000 inhabitants

Capital cities are denoted by capital letter

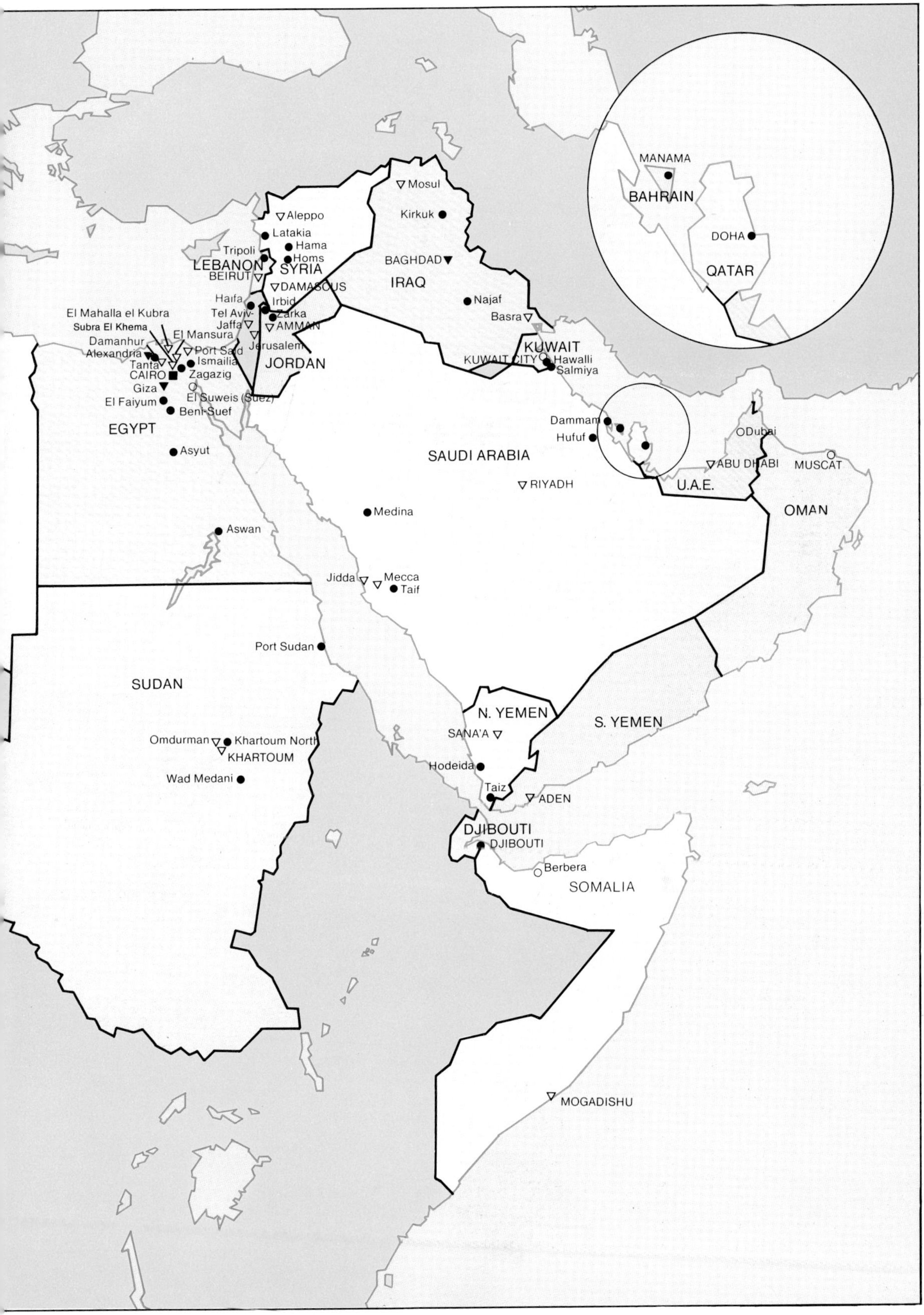
MANAMA
BAHRAIN
DOHA
QATAR
Mosul
Aleppo
Kirkuk
Latakia
Hama
Tripoli
Homs
LEBANON
SYRIA
BEIRUT
BAGHDAD
DAMASCUS
IRAQ
Haifa
Irbid
Najaf
El Mahalla el Kubra
Tel Aviv-Jaffa
Zarka
Subra El Khema
AMMAN
Basra
Damanhur
El Mansura
Jerusalem
KUWAIT
Alexandria
Port Said
Ismailia
JORDAN
KUWAIT CITY
Hawalli
Salmiya
Tanta
CAIRO
Zagazig
Giza
El Suweis (Suez)
El Faiyum
Beni-Suef
Dammam
EGYPT
Hufuf
Dubai
Asyut
SAUDI ARABIA
ABU DHABI
MUSCAT
RIYADH
U.A.E.
Medina
OMAN
Aswan
Jidda
Mecca
Taif
Port Sudan
SUDAN
N. YEMEN
S. YEMEN
SANA'A
Omdurman
Khartoum North
KHARTOUM
Hodeida
Wad Medani
Taiz
ADEN
DJIBOUTI
DJIBOUTI
Berbera
SOMALIA
MOGADISHU

2 The Shape of the Land

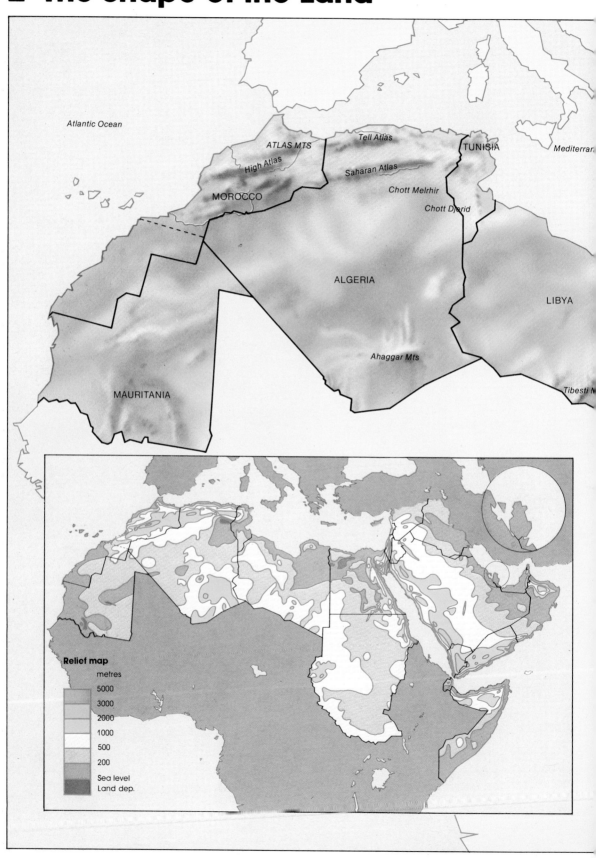

Atlantic Ocean

ATLAS MTS
High Atlas
Tell Atlas
Saharan Atlas
TUNISIA
Mediterrar.
Chott Melrhir
MOROCCO
Chott Djerid

ALGERIA

LIBYA

Ahaggar Mts

MAURITANIA

Tibesti M

Relief map

metres

5000
3000
2000
1000
500
200
Sea level
Land dep.

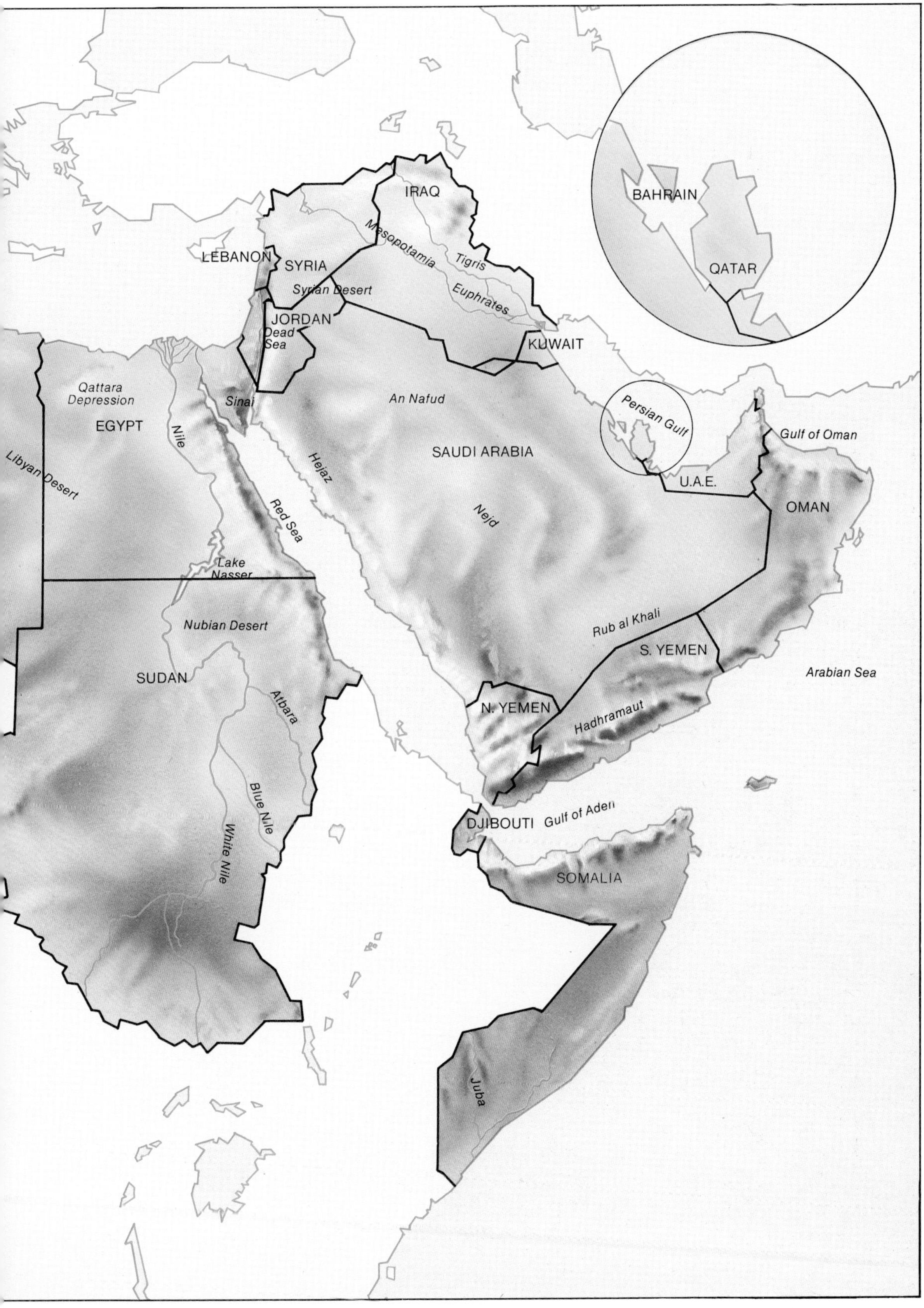

IRAQ
BAHRAIN
QATAR
LEBANON
SYRIA
Mesopotamia
Tigris
Syrian Desert
Euphrates
JORDAN
Dead Sea
KUWAIT
Qattara Depression
Sinai
An Nafud
Persian Gulf
EGYPT
Nile
Gulf of Oman
Libyan Desert
Hejaz
SAUDI ARABIA
U.A.E.
Red Sea
Nejd
OMAN
Lake Nasser
Nubian Desert
Rub al Khali
S. YEMEN
SUDAN
Arabian Sea
Atbara
N. YEMEN
Hadhramaut
Blue Nile
White Nile
DJIBOUTI
Gulf of Aden
SOMALIA
Juba

3 Temperature and Insolation

Mean January temperature

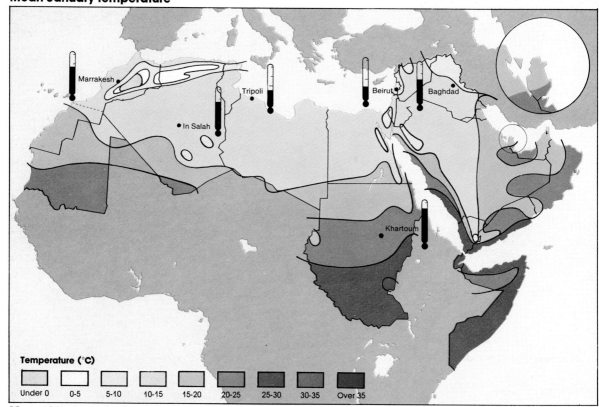

Temperature (°C)

Under 0	0-5	5-10	10-15	15-20	20-25	25-30	30-35	Over 35

Mean July temperature

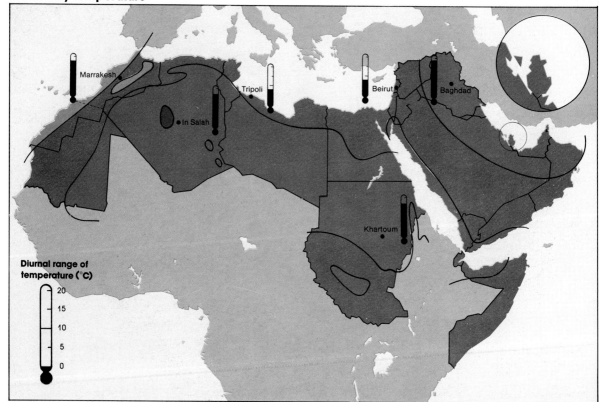

Diurnal range of
temperature (°C)

20
15
10
5
0

Mean annual hours of sunshine

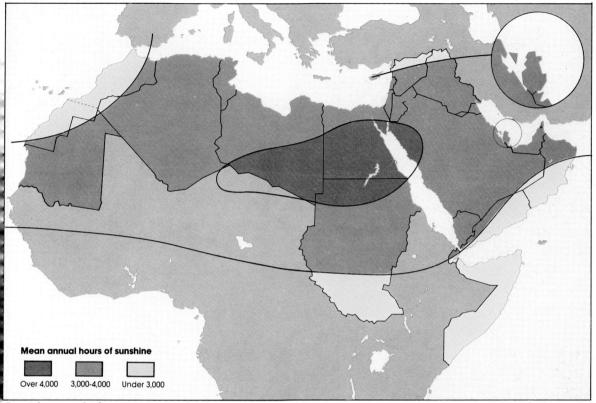

Mean annual hours of sunshine

Over 4,000	3,000-4,000	Under 3,000

Frost-free period

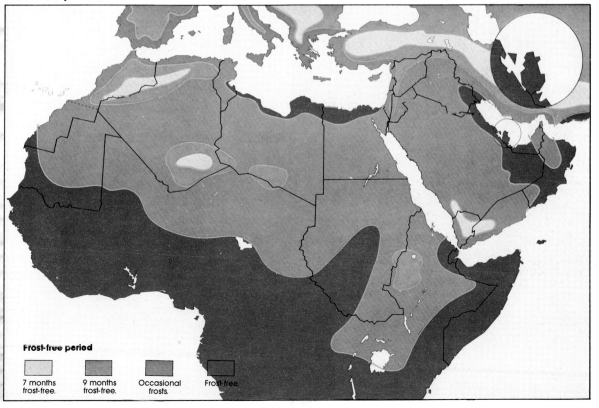

Frost-free period

7 months frost-free.	9 months frost-free.	Occasional frosts.	Frost-free.

4 Winds and Rainfall

Pressure and prevailing winds January

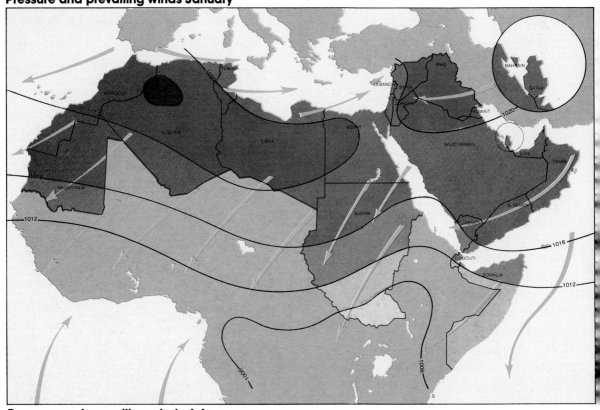

Pressure and prevailing winds July

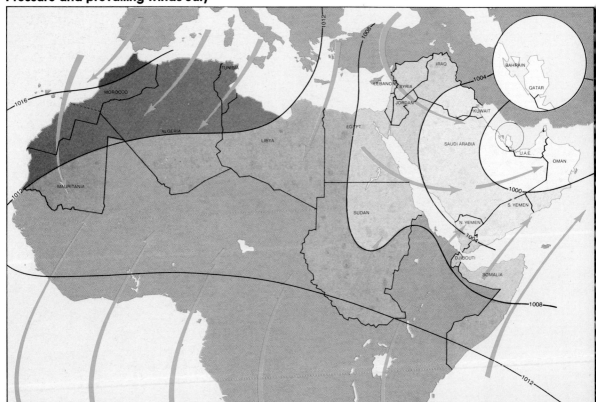

Mean annual precipitation

BAHRAIN

QATAR

OMAN

U.A.E.

S. YEMEN

N. YEMEN

SAUDI ARABIA

Kuwait ·
KUWAIT

Mosul ·
IRAQ

SYRIA

JORDAN

LEBANON
Beirut ·

Port Said ·

EGYPT

Asyut ·

Jidda ·

Khartoum ·

SUDAN

Juba ·

DJIBOUTI
Berbera ·

SOMALIA

Mogadishu ·

Tripoli ·

LIBYA

TUNISIA

Tamanrasset ·

ALGERIA

MOROCCO

Casablanca ·

MAURITANIA

Nouadhibou ·

Mean annual precipitation

Under 100 mm

100-250 mm

250-500 mm

500-1,000 mm

Over 1,000 mm

**Seasonal distribution
of precipitation**

November-April

May-October

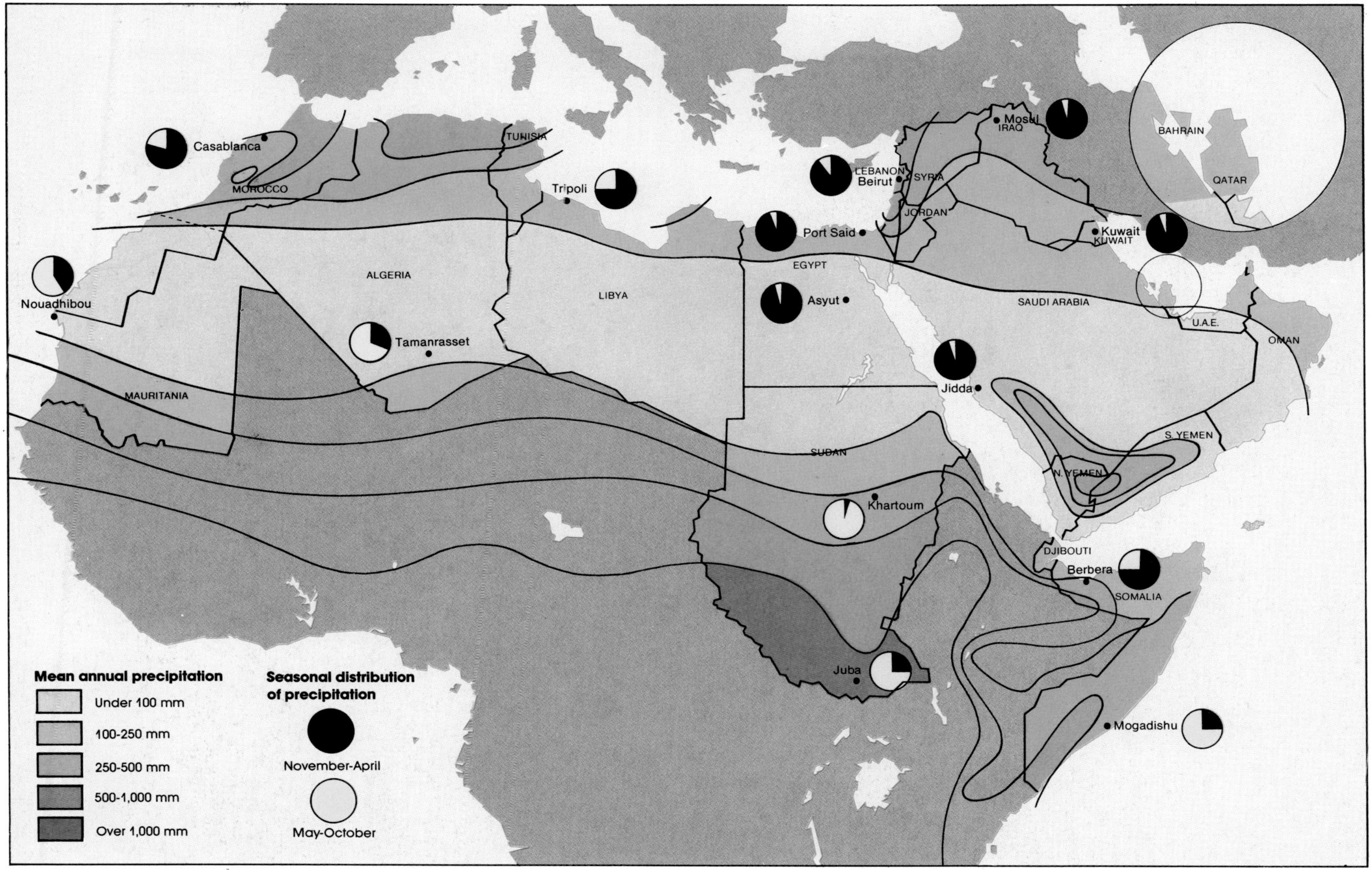

5 Natural Vegetation

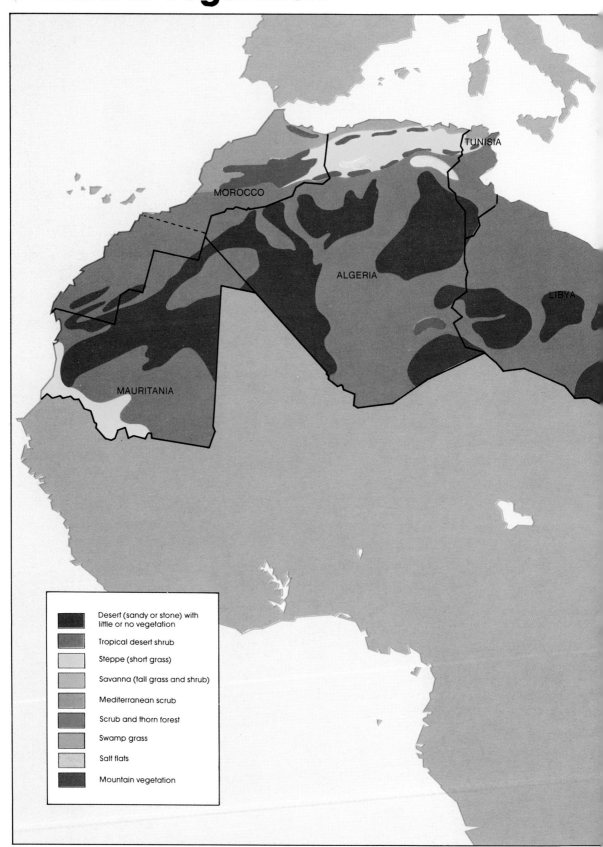

TUNISIA

MOROCCO

ALGERIA

LIBYA

MAURITANIA

Desert (sandy or stone) with
little or no vegetation

Tropical desert shrub

Steppe (short grass)

Savanna (tall grass and shrub)

Mediterranean scrub

Scrub and thorn forest

Swamp grass

Salt flats

Mountain vegetation

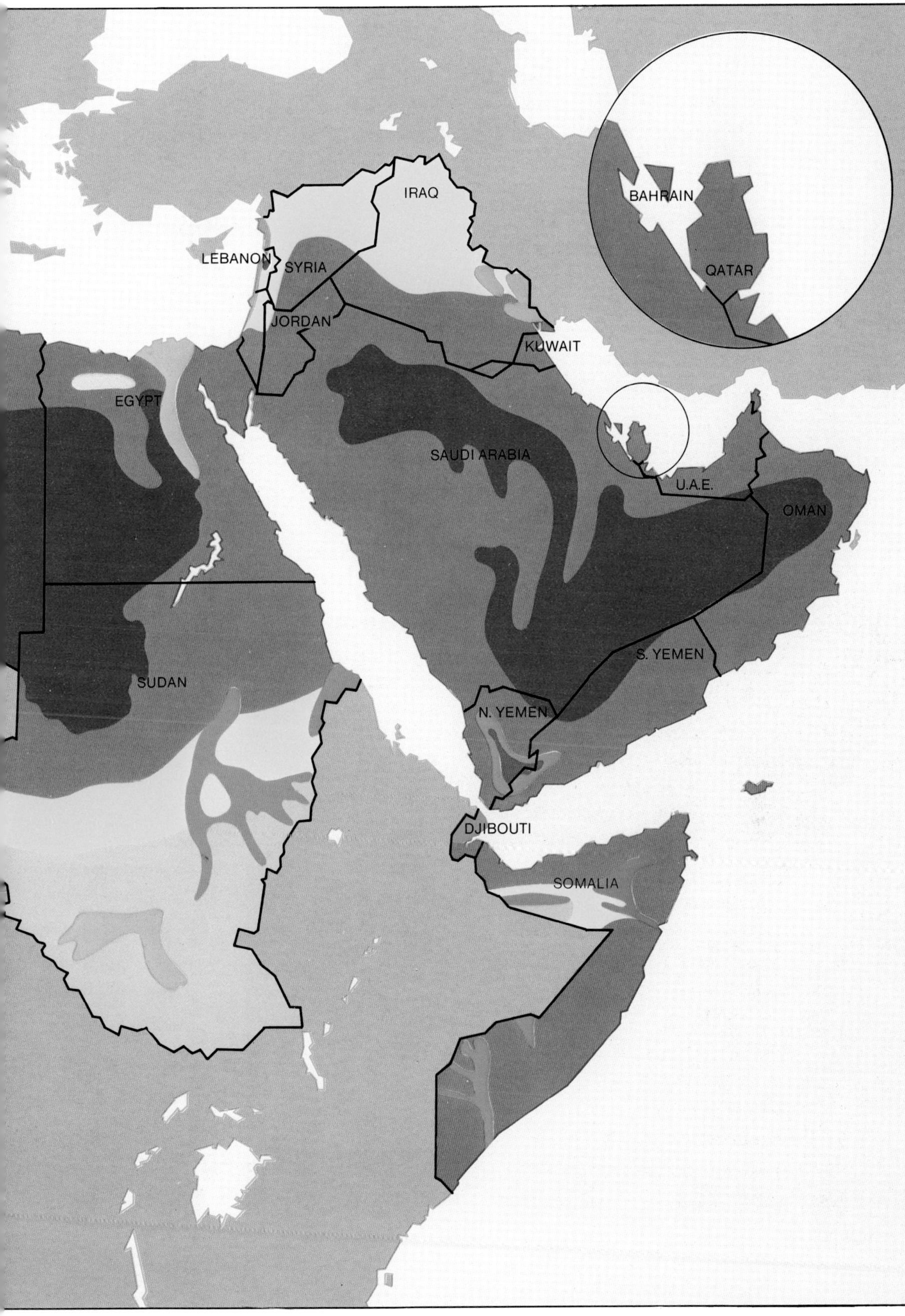
IRAQ
BAHRAIN
LEBANON
SYRIA
QATAR
JORDAN
KUWAIT
EGYPT
SAUDI ARABIA
U.A.E.
OMAN
S. YEMEN
SUDAN
N. YEMEN
DJIBOUTI
SOMALIA

6 Population

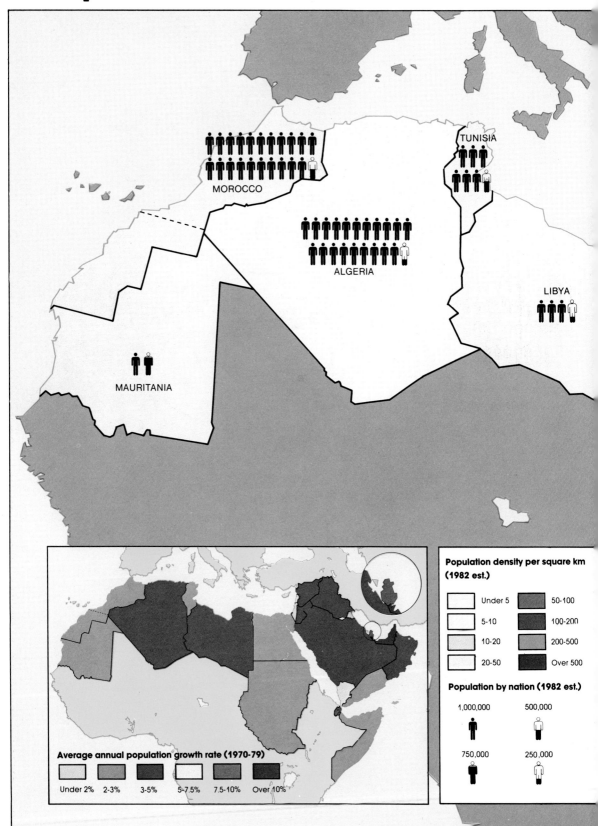

MOROCCO

TUNISIA

ALGERIA

LIBYA

MAURITANIA

Population density per square km (1982 est.)

Under 5		50-100	
5-10		100-200	
10-20		200-500	
20-50		Over 500	

Population by nation (1982 est.)

1,000,000   500,000

750,000   250,000

Average annual population growth rate (1970-79)

Under 2%   2-3%   3-5%   5-7.5%   7.5-10%   Over 10%

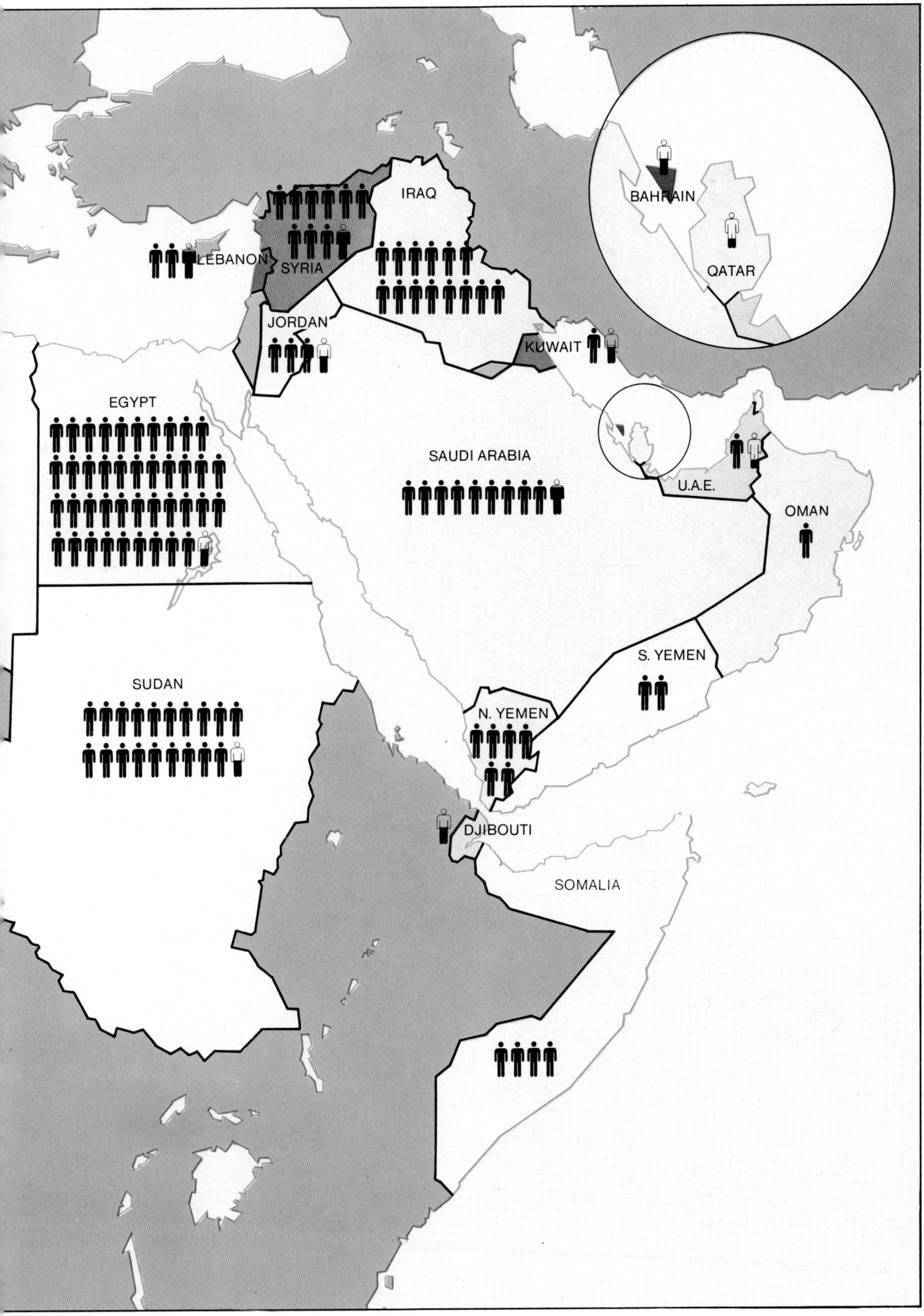

IRAQ
BAHRAIN
QATAR
LEBANON
SYRIA
JORDAN
KUWAIT
EGYPT
SAUDI ARABIA
U.A.E.
OMAN
S. YEMEN
SUDAN
N. YEMEN
DJIBOUTI
SOMALIA

7 Health and Medical Care

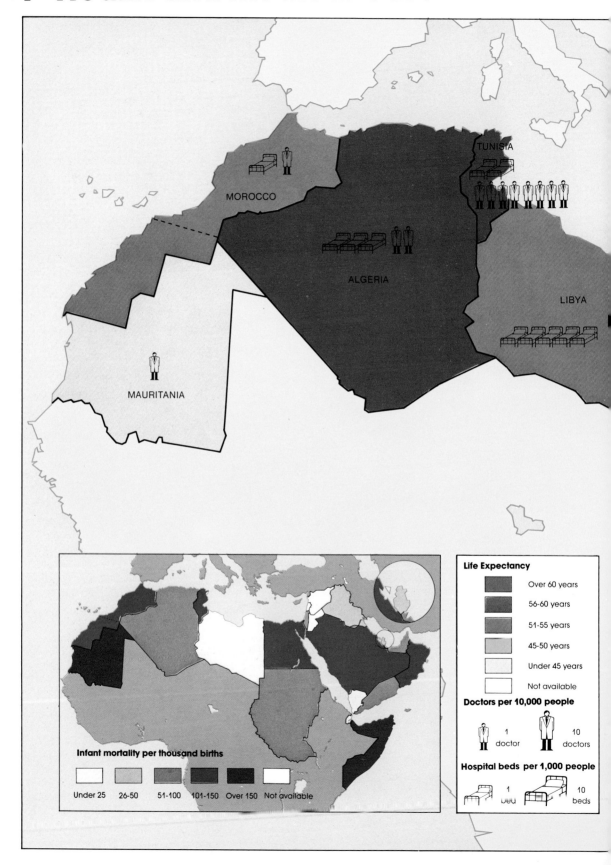

MOROCCO

TUNISIA

ALGERIA

LIBYA

MAURITANIA

Life Expectancy

Over 60 years

56-60 years

51-55 years

45-50 years

Under 45 years

Not available

Doctors per 10,000 people

1 doctor

10 doctors

Hospital beds per 1,000 people

1 bed

10 beds

Infant mortality per thousand births

Under 25   26-50   51-100   101-150   Over 150   Not available

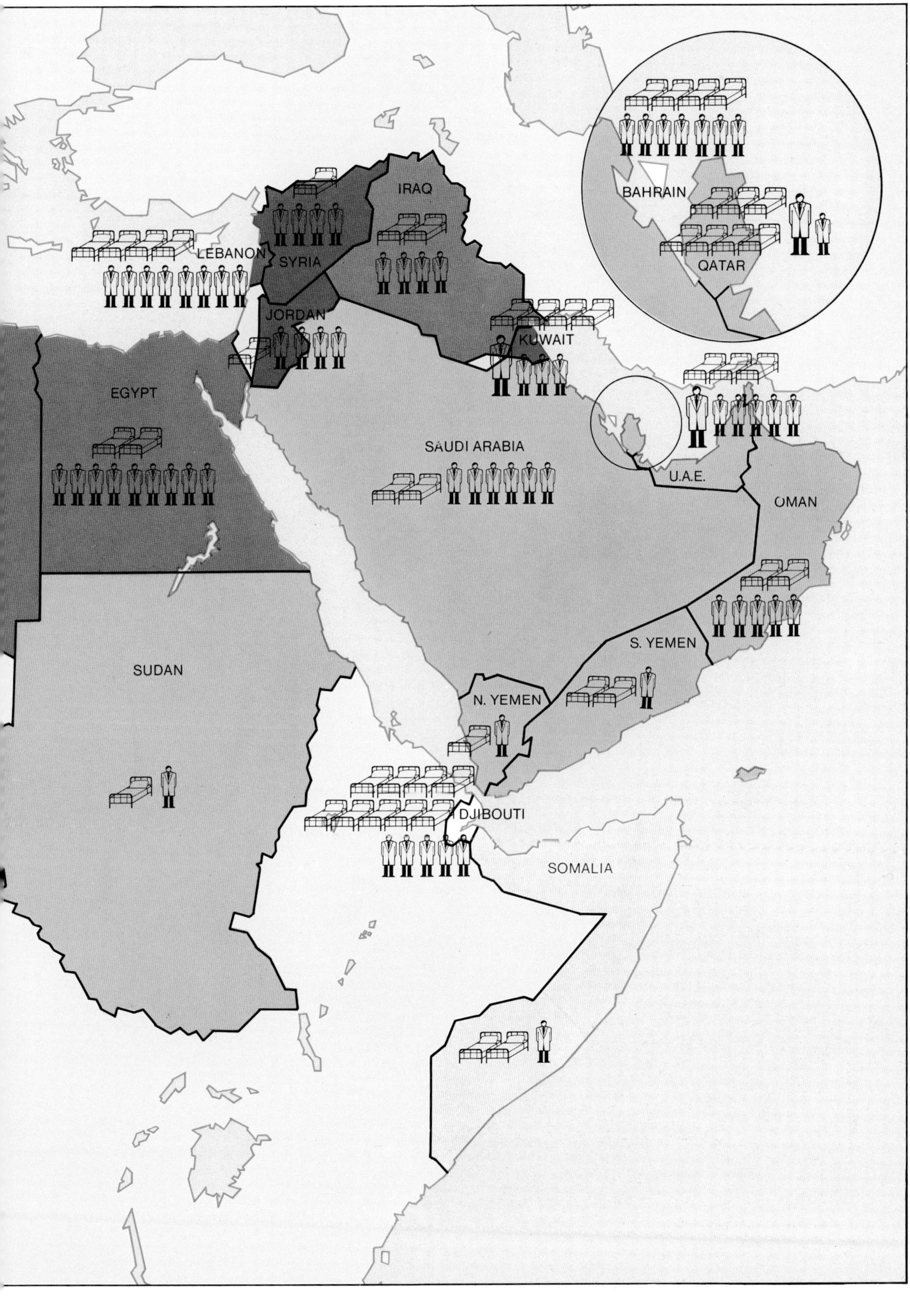

LEBANON
SYRIA
IRAQ
JORDAN
KUWAIT
BAHRAIN
QATAR
EGYPT
SAUDI ARABIA
U.A.E.
OMAN
S. YEMEN
N. YEMEN
SUDAN
DJIBOUTI
SOMALIA

8 Food and Nutrition

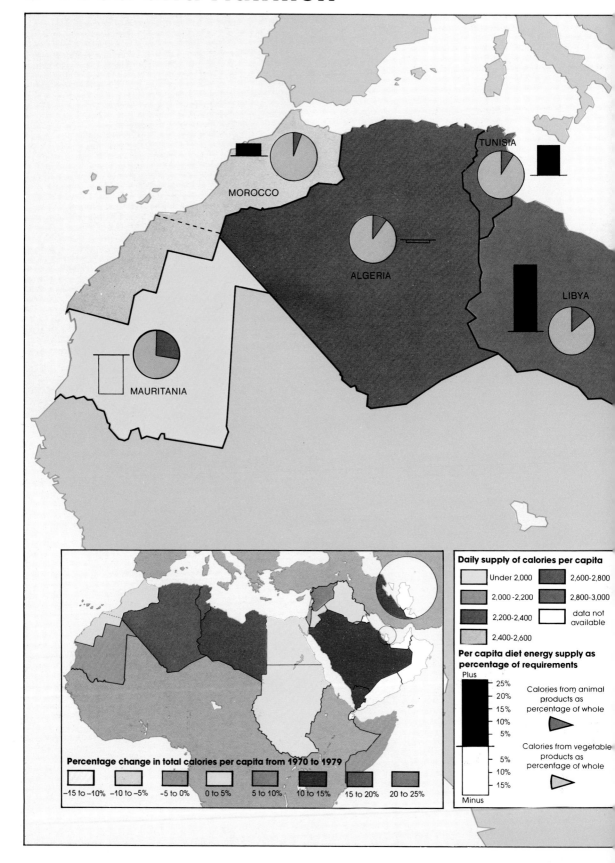

MOROCCO

TUNISIA

ALGERIA

LIBYA

MAURITANIA

Daily supply of calories per capita

Under 2,000	2,600-2,800
2,000-2,200	2,800-3,000
2,200-2,400	data not available
2,400-2,600	

Per capita diet energy supply as percentage of requirements

Plus
- 25%
- 20%
- 15%
- 10%
- 5%

Calories from animal products as percentage of whole

- 5%
- 10%
- 15%

Minus

Calories from vegetable products as percentage of whole

Percentage change in total calories per capita from 1970 to 1979

-15 to -10%	-10 to -5%	-5 to 0%	0 to 5%	5 to 10%	10 to 15%	15 to 20%	20 to 25%

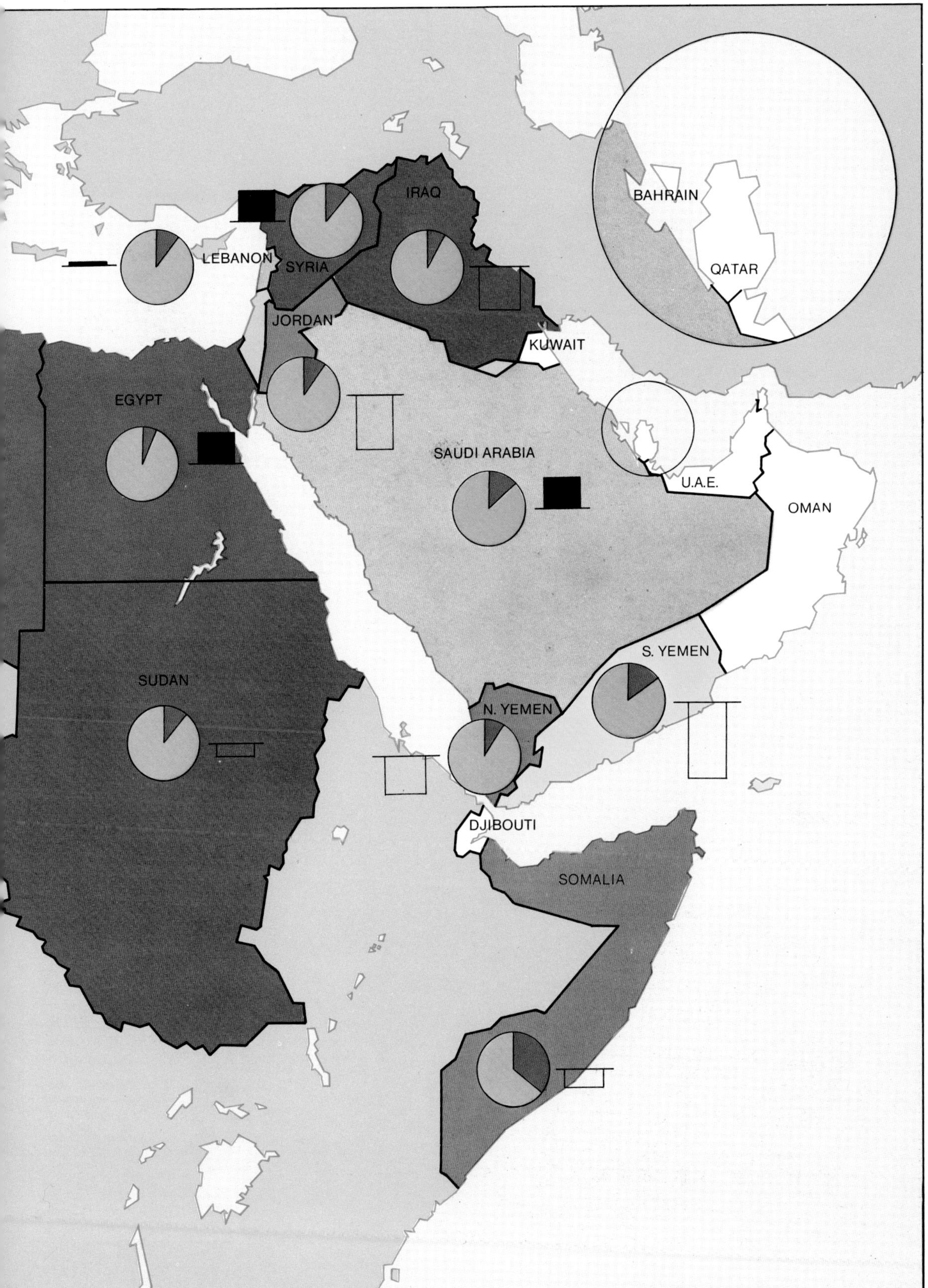
BAHRAIN
QATAR
IRAQ
LEBANON
SYRIA
JORDAN
KUWAIT
EGYPT
SAUDI ARABIA
U.A.E.
OMAN
S. YEMEN
SUDAN
N. YEMEN
DJIBOUTI
SOMALIA

9 Literacy and Learning

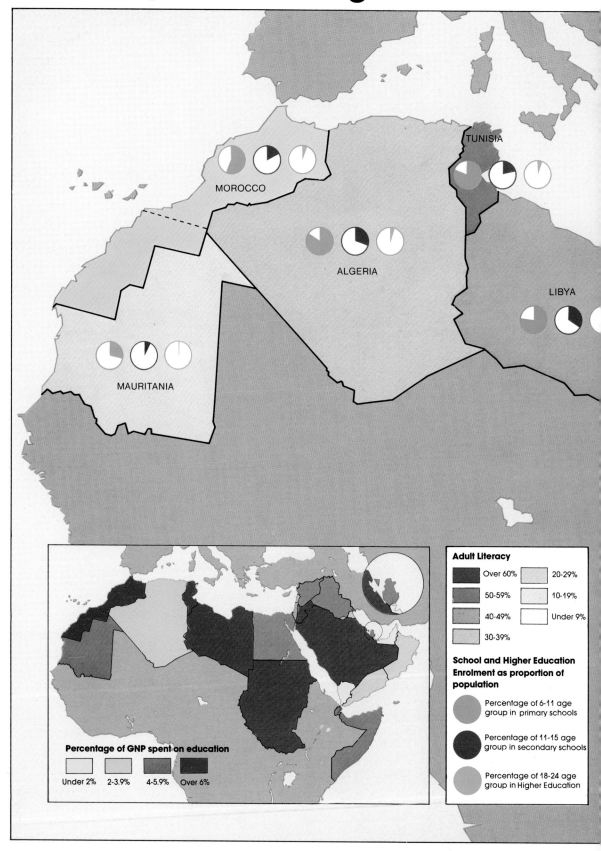

MOROCCO

TUNISIA

ALGERIA

LIBYA

MAURITANIA

Adult Literacy

Over 60%	20-29%
50-59%	10-19%
40-49%	Under 9%
30-39%	

School and Higher Education Enrolment as proportion of population

Percentage of 6-11 age group in primary schools

Percentage of 11-15 age group in secondary schools

Percentage of 18-24 age group in Higher Education

Percentage of GNP spent on education

Under 2% 2-3.9% 4-5.9% Over 6%

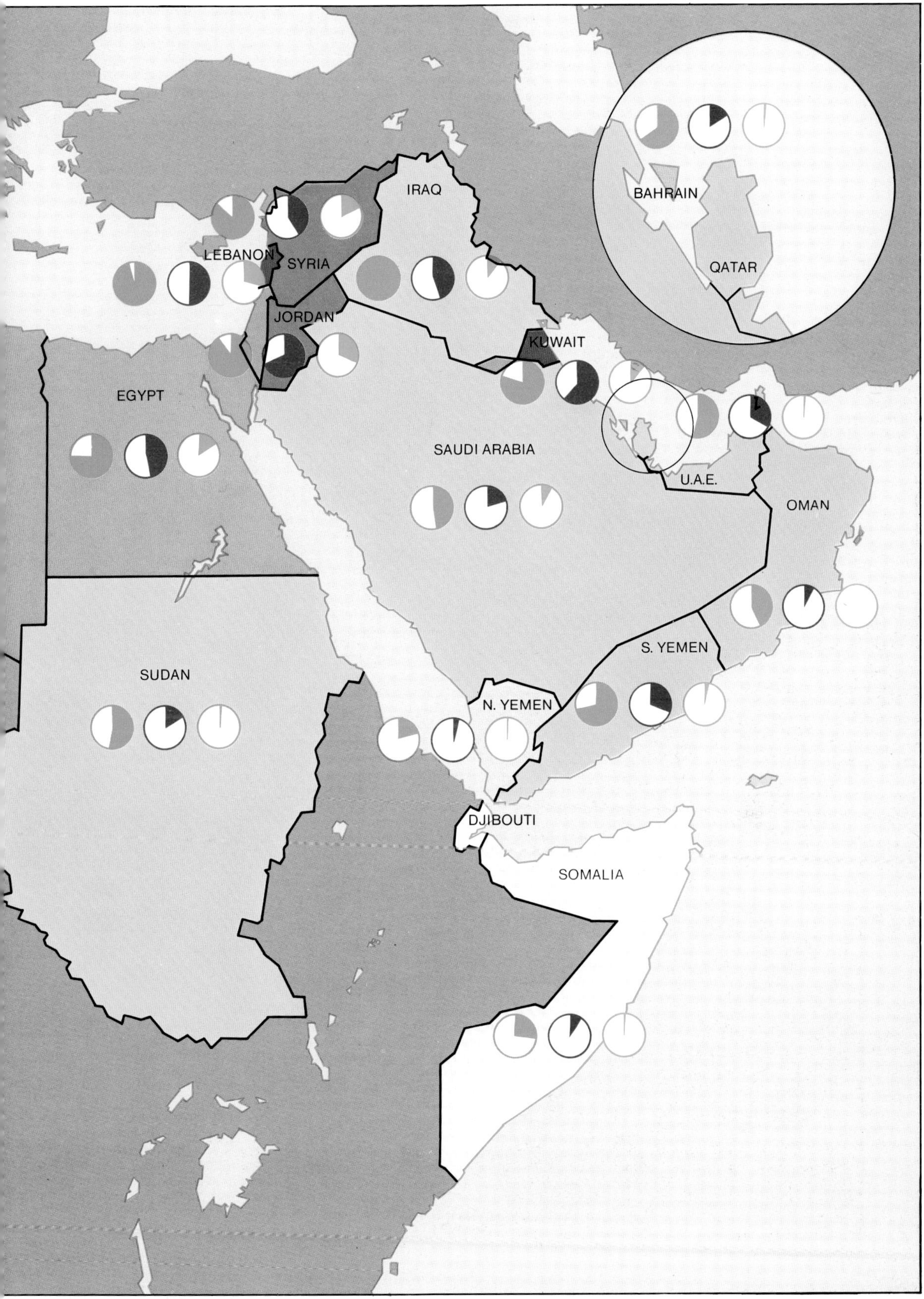

IRAQ
BAHRAIN
QATAR
LEBANON
SYRIA
JORDAN
KUWAIT
EGYPT
SAUDI ARABIA
U.A.E.
OMAN
S. YEMEN
SUDAN
N. YEMEN
DJIBOUTI
SOMALIA

10 Standard of Living

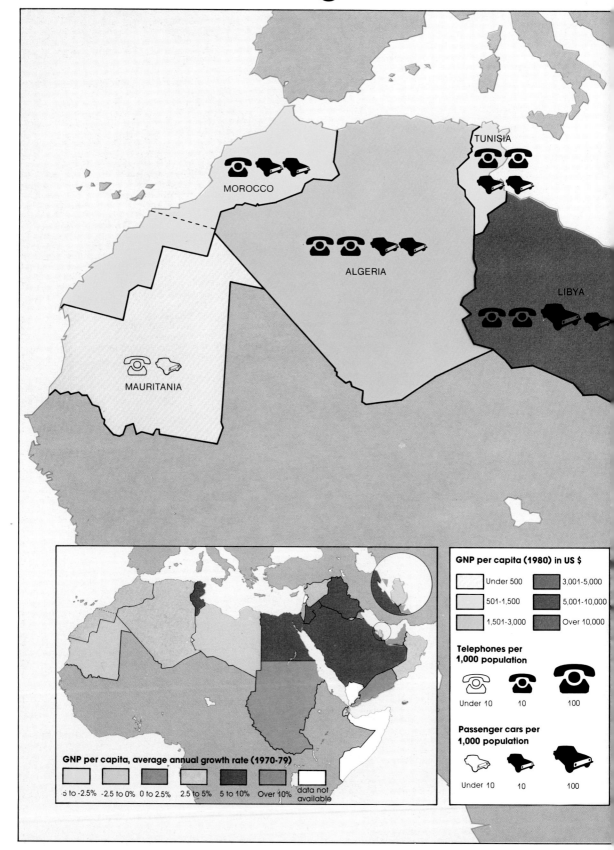

MOROCCO

TUNISIA

ALGERIA

LIBYA

MAURITANIA

GNP per capita (1980) in US $

Under 500

501-1,500

1,501-3,000

3,001-5,000

5,001-10,000

Over 10,000

Telephones per 1,000 population

Under 10

10

100

Passenger cars per 1,000 population

Under 10

10

100

GNP per capita, average annual growth rate (1970-79)

5 to -2.5%   -2.5 to 0%   0 to 2.5%   2.5 to 5%   5 to 10%   Over 10%   data not available

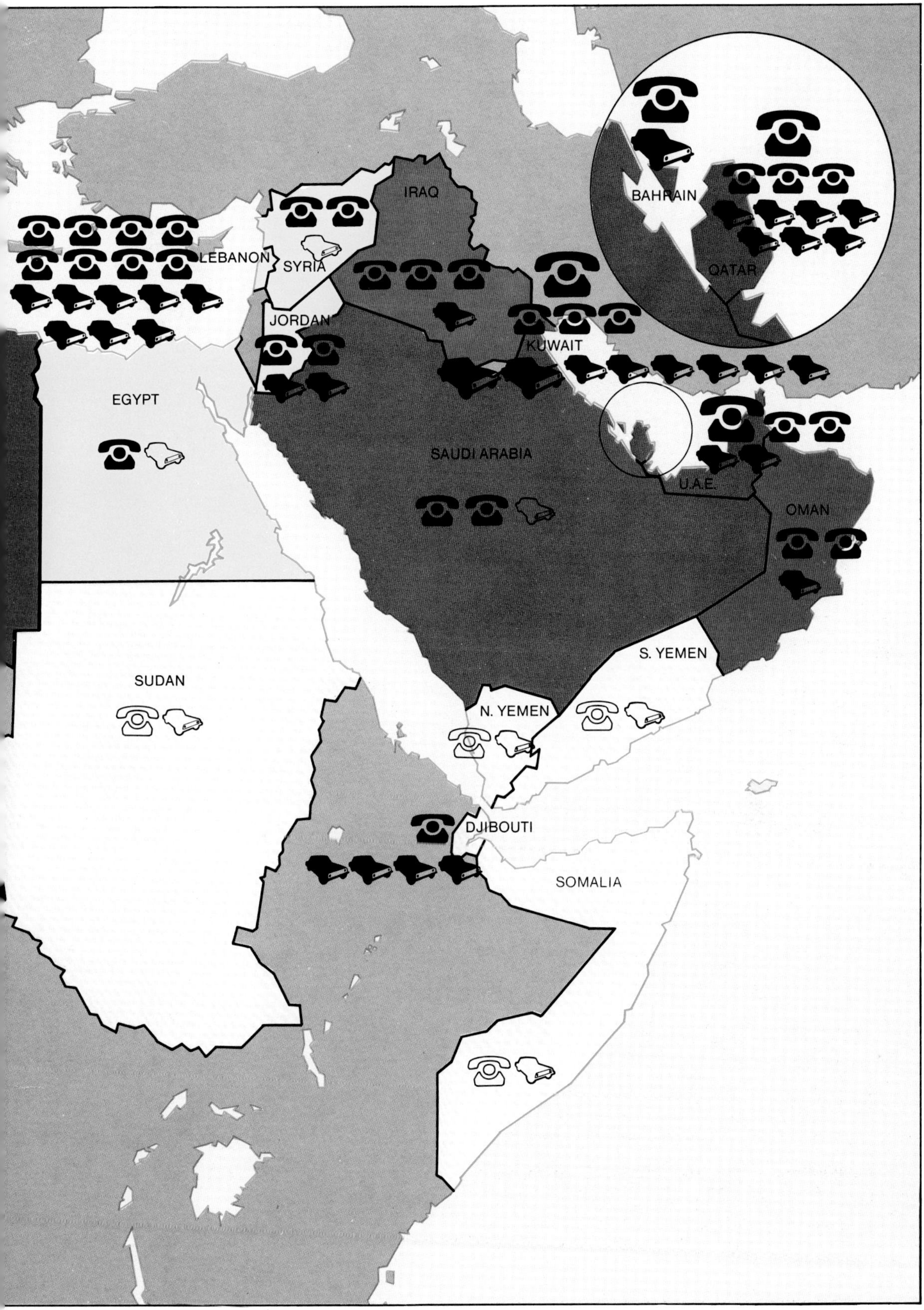

IRAQ
BAHRAIN
LEBANON
SYRIA
QATAR
JORDAN
KUWAIT
EGYPT
SAUDI ARABIA
U.A.E.
OMAN
S. YEMEN
SUDAN
N. YEMEN
DJIBOUTI
SOMALIA

11 Living Standards Compared

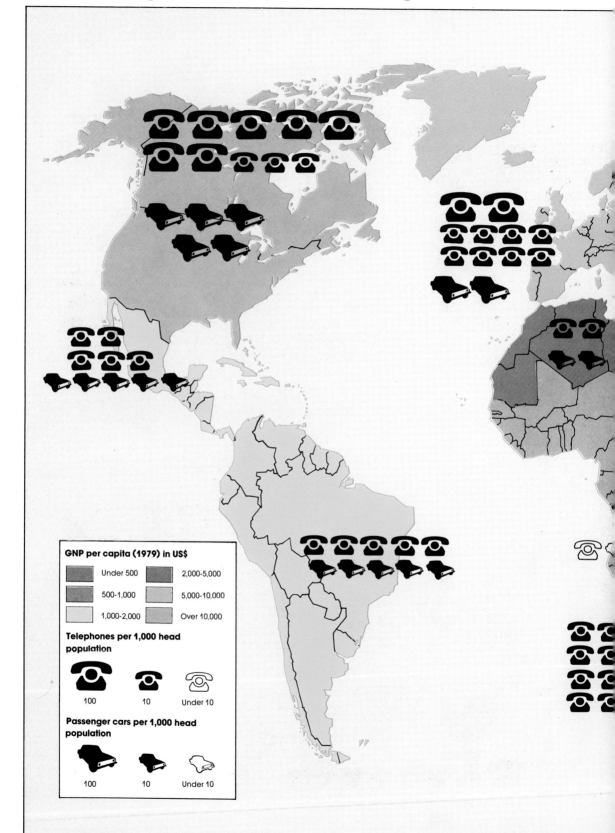

GNP per capita (1979) in US$

Under 500	2,000-5,000
500-1,000	5,000-10,000
1,000-2,000	Over 10,000

Telephones per 1,000 head population

100   10   Under 10

Passenger cars per 1,000 head population

100   10   Under 10

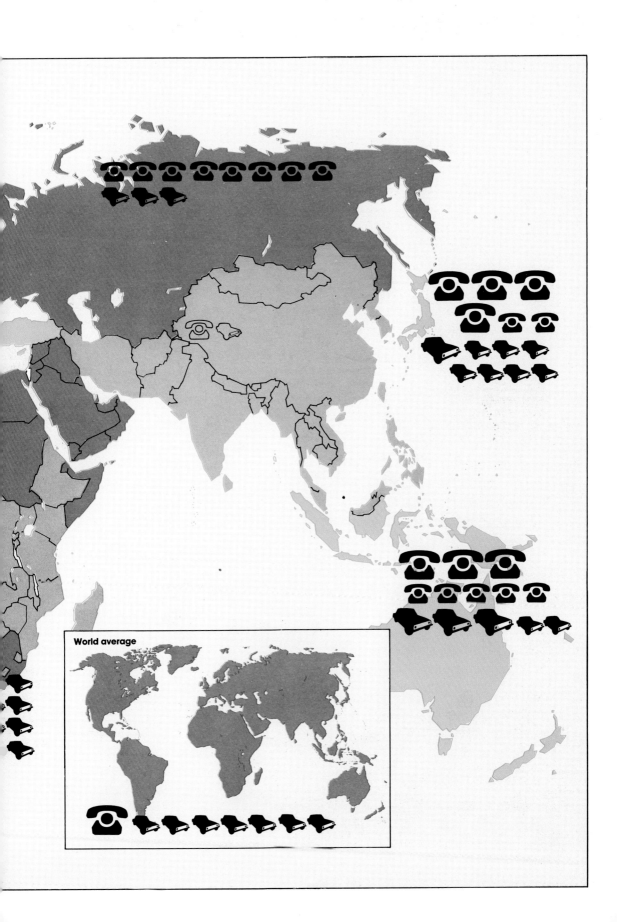

World average

12 Employment

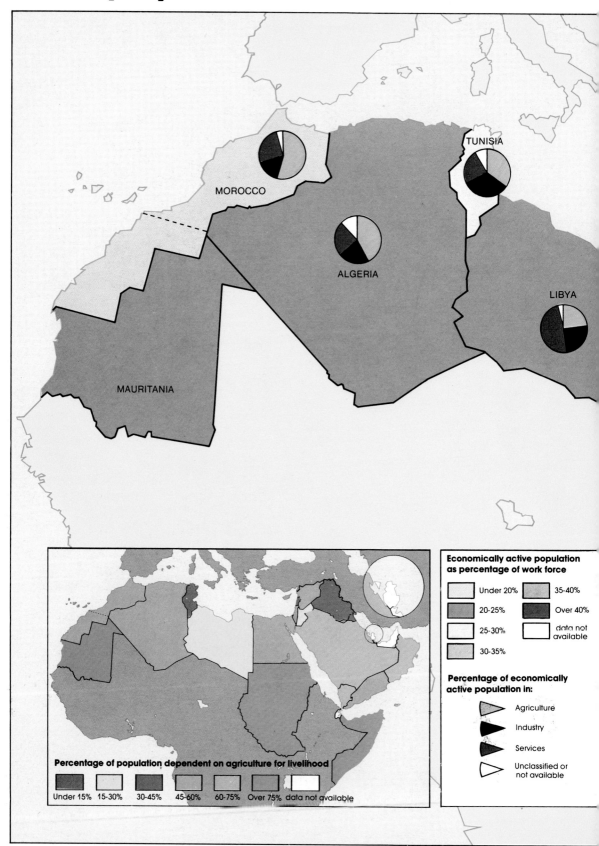

MOROCCO

TUNISIA

ALGERIA

LIBYA

MAURITANIA

Economically active population as percentage of work force

- Under 20%
- 20-25%
- 25-30%
- 30-35%
- 35-40%
- Over 40%
- data not available

Percentage of economically active population in:

- Agriculture
- Industry
- Services
- Unclassified or not available

Percentage of population dependent on agriculture for livelihood

Under 15%   15-30%   30-45%   45-60%   60-75%   Over 75%   data not available

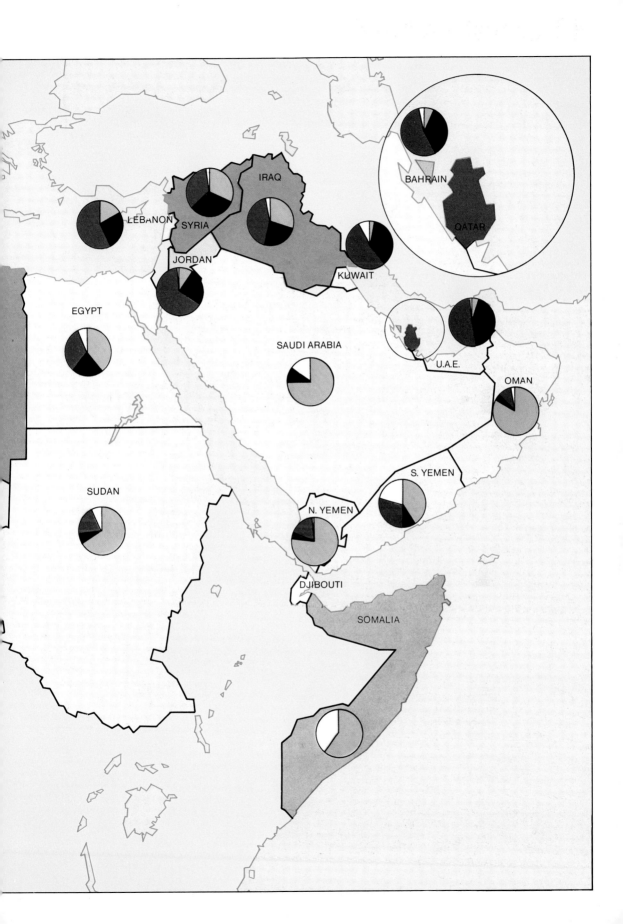

LEBANON

SYRIA

IRAQ

BAHRAIN

QATAR

JORDAN

KUWAIT

EGYPT

SAUDI ARABIA

U.A.E.

OMAN

SUDAN

S. YEMEN

N. YEMEN

DJIBOUTI

SOMALIA

13 Land Use

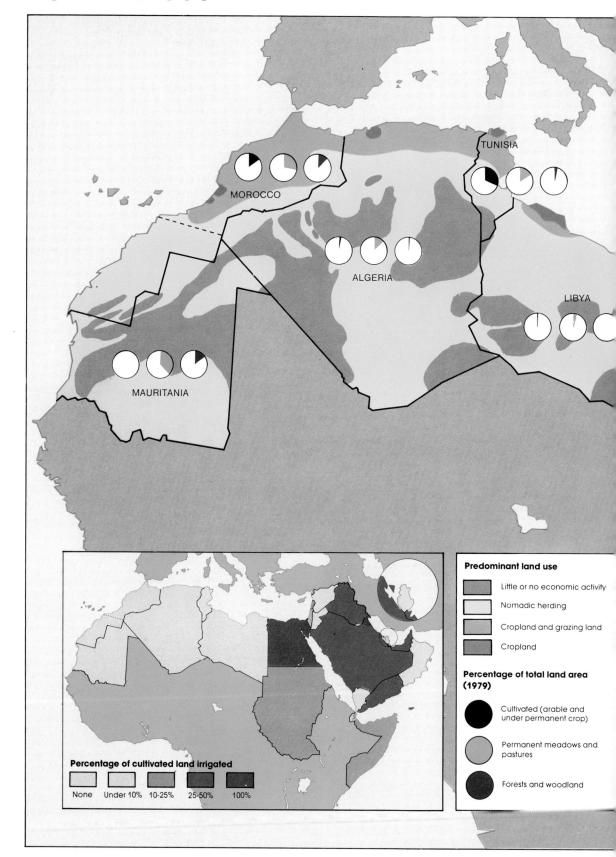

TUNISIA

MOROCCO

ALGERIA

LIBYA

MAURITANIA

Predominant land use

- Little or no economic activity
- Nomadic herding
- Cropland and grazing land
- Cropland

Percentage of total land area (1979)

- Cultivated (arable and under permanent crop)
- Permanent meadows and pastures
- Forests and woodland

Percentage of cultivated land irrigated

| None | Under 10% | 10-25% | 25-50% | 100% |

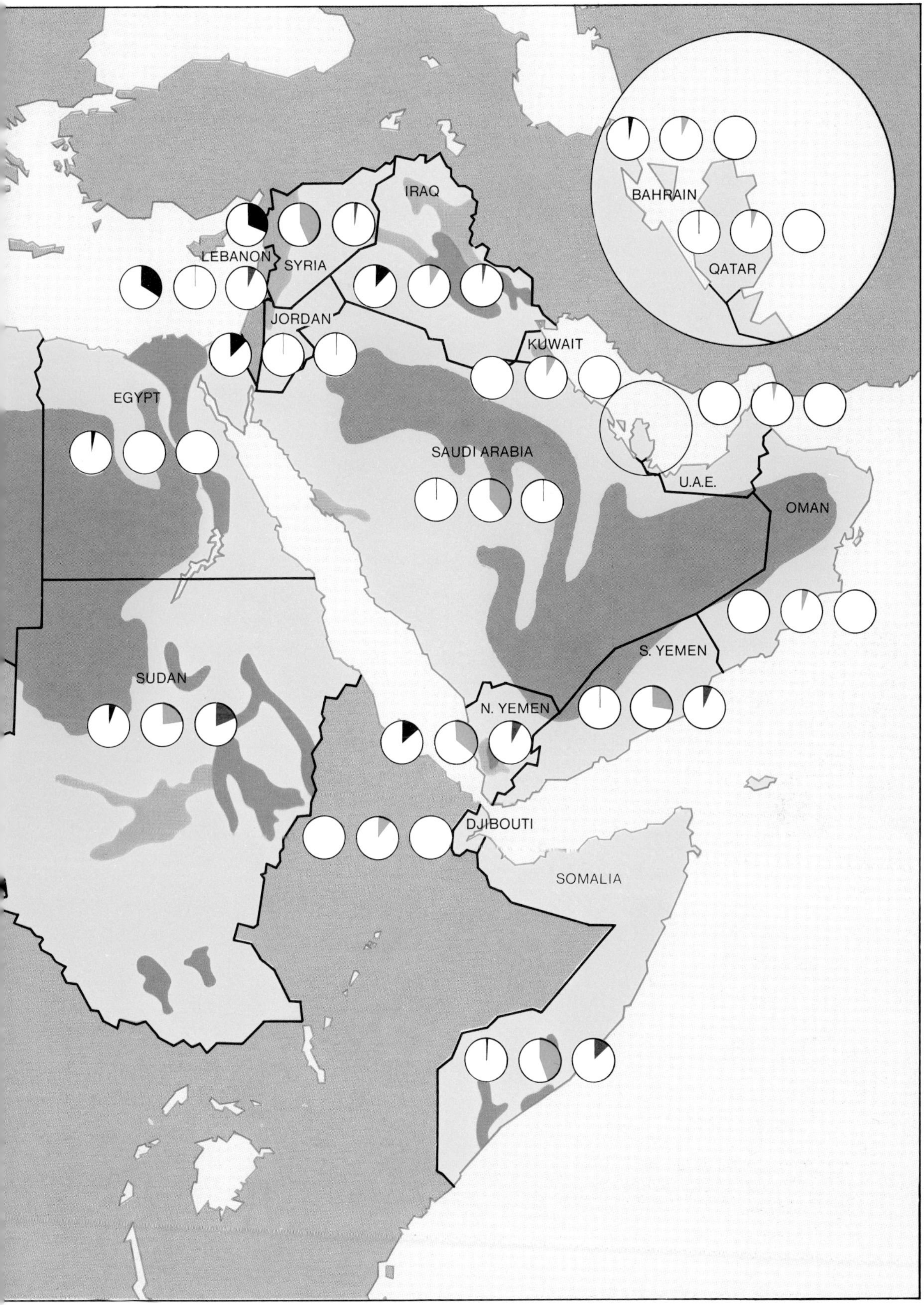

IRAQ
BAHRAIN
QATAR
LEBANON
SYRIA
JORDAN
KUWAIT
EGYPT
SAUDI ARABIA
U.A.E.
OMAN
S. YEMEN
SUDAN
N. YEMEN
DJIBOUTI
SOMALIA

14 Agriculture

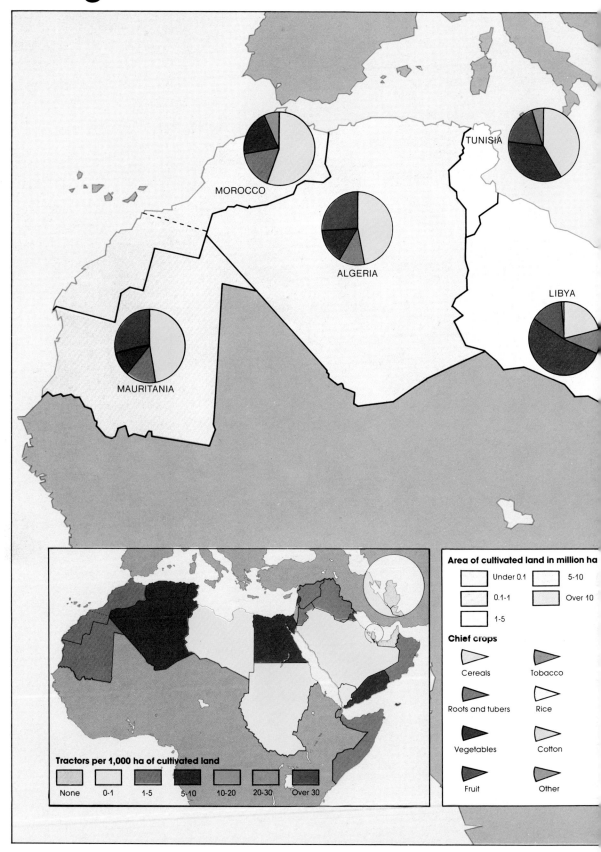

TUNISIA

MOROCCO

ALGERIA

LIBYA

MAURITANIA

Area of cultivated land in million ha

Under 0.1		5-10
0.1-1		Over 10
1-5		

Chief crops

Cereals

Tobacco

Roots and tubers

Rice

Vegetables

Cotton

Fruit

Other

Tractors per 1,000 ha of cultivated land

None	0-1	1-5	5-10	10-20	20-30	Over 30

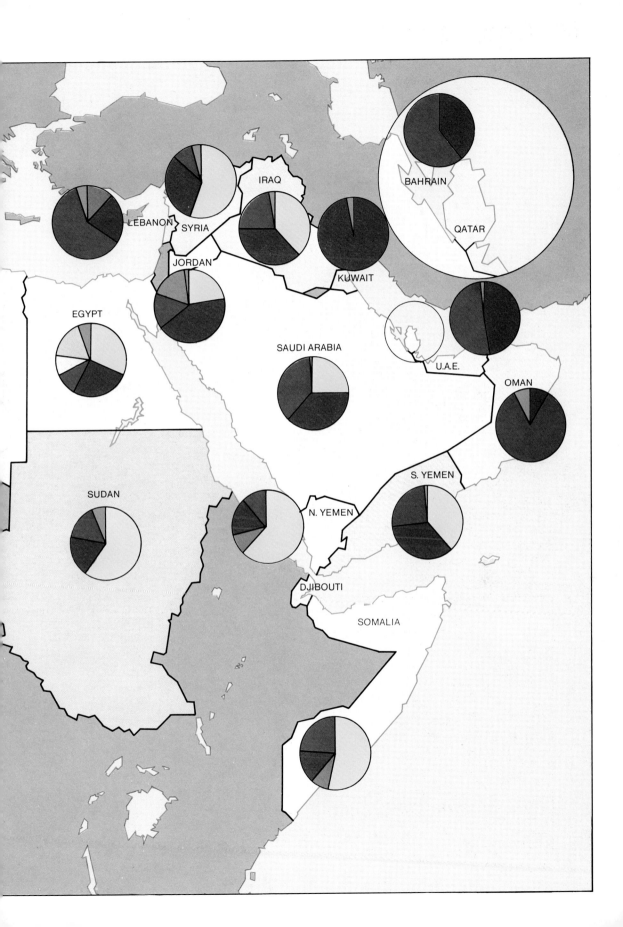

LEBANON

SYRIA

IRAQ

BAHRAIN

QATAR

JORDAN

EGYPT

SAUDI ARABIA

KUWAIT

U.A.E.

OMAN

SUDAN

N. YEMEN

S. YEMEN

DJIBOUTI

SOMALIA

15 Livestock

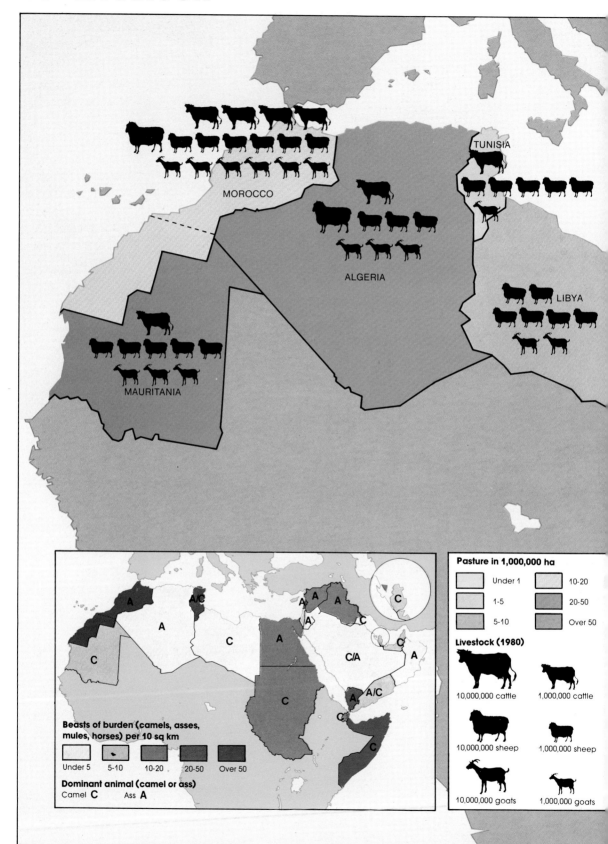

MOROCCO

TUNISIA

ALGERIA

LIBYA

MAURITANIA

Pasture in 1,000,000 ha

Under 1	10-20
1-5	20-50
5-10	Over 50

Livestock (1980)

10,000,000 cattle	1,000,000 cattle
10,000,000 sheep	1,000,000 sheep
10,000,000 goats	1,000,000 goats

Beasts of burden (camels, asses, mules, horses) per 10 sq km

Under 5	5-10	10-20	20-50	Over 50

Dominant animal (camel or ass)

Camel **C**   Ass **A**

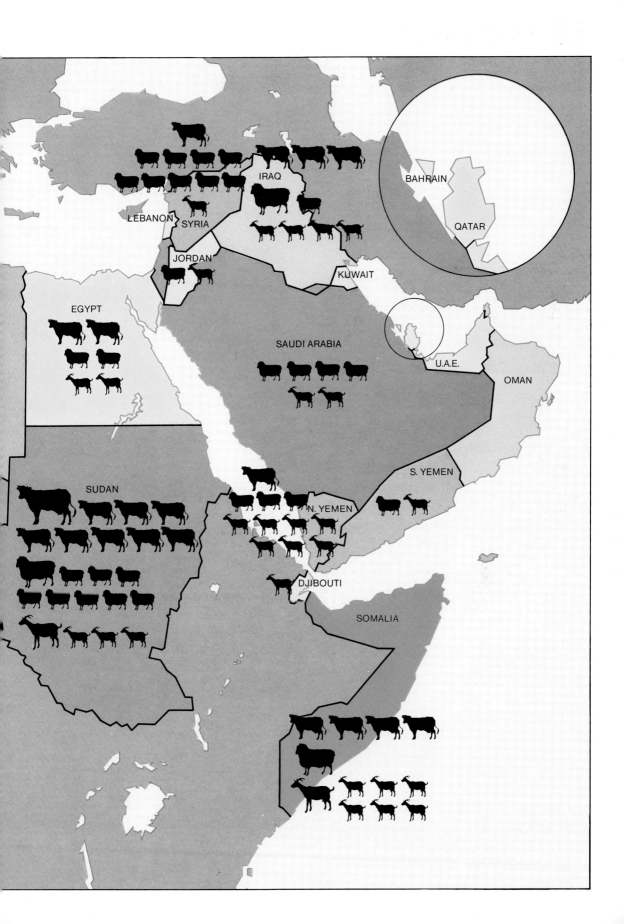

BAHRAIN

QATAR

IRAQ

LEBANON

SYRIA

JORDAN

KUWAIT

EGYPT

SAUDI ARABIA

U.A.E.

OMAN

S. YEMEN

SUDAN

N. YEMEN

DJIBOUTI

SOMALIA

16 The Balance of Farming

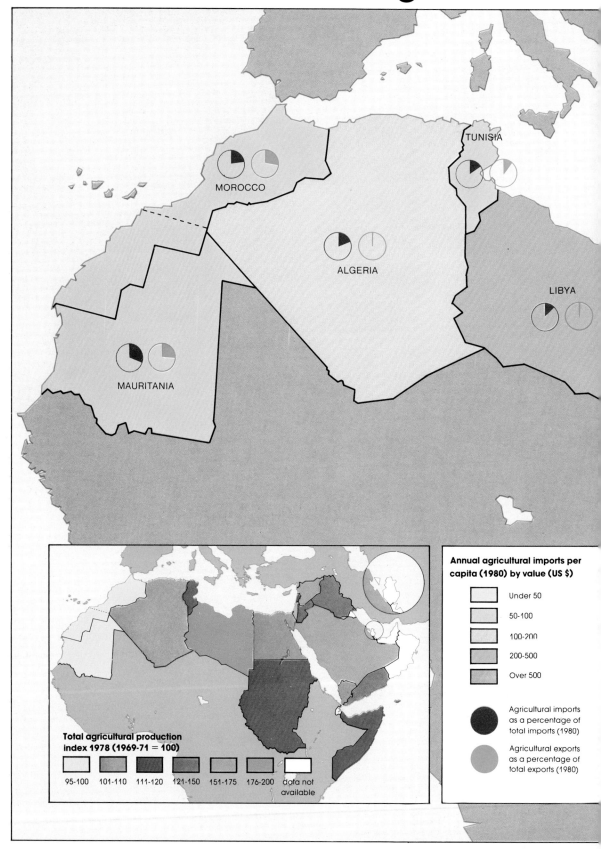

TUNISIA

MOROCCO

ALGERIA

LIBYA

MAURITANIA

Annual agricultural imports per capita (1980) by value (US $)

Under 50

50-100

100-200

200-500

Over 500

Agricultural imports as a percentage of total imports (1980)

Agricultural exports as a percentage of total exports (1980)

Total agricultural production index 1978 (1969-71 = 100)

95-100 101-110 111-120 121-150 151-175 176-200 data not available

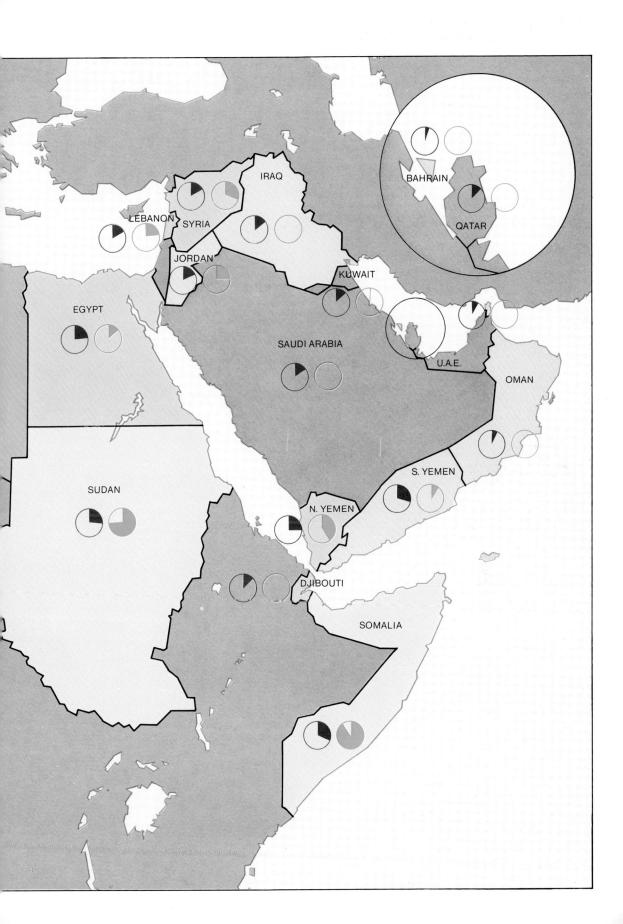

LEBANON
SYRIA
IRAQ
JORDAN
KUWAIT
BAHRAIN
QATAR
U.A.E.
EGYPT
SAUDI ARABIA
OMAN
SUDAN
S. YEMEN
N. YEMEN
DJIBOUTI
SOMALIA

17 Mineral Wealth

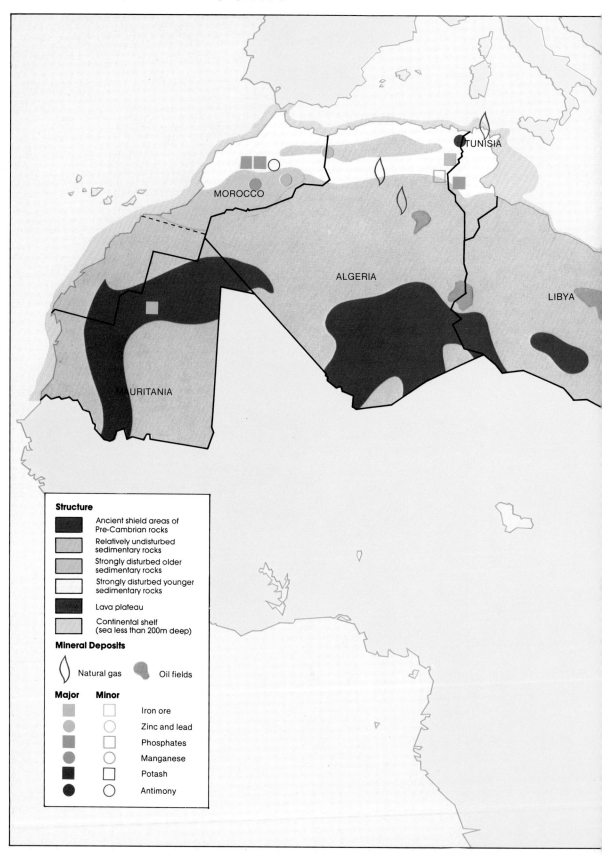

Structure

- Ancient shield areas of Pre-Cambrian rocks
- Relatively undisturbed sedimentary rocks
- Strongly disturbed older sedimentary rocks
- Strongly disturbed younger sedimentary rocks
- Lava plateau
- Continental shelf (sea less than 200m deep)

Mineral Deposits

- Natural gas
- Oil fields

Major	Minor	
		Iron ore
		Zinc and lead
		Phosphates
		Manganese
		Potash
		Antimony

MOROCCO

ALGERIA

TUNISIA

LIBYA

MAURITANIA

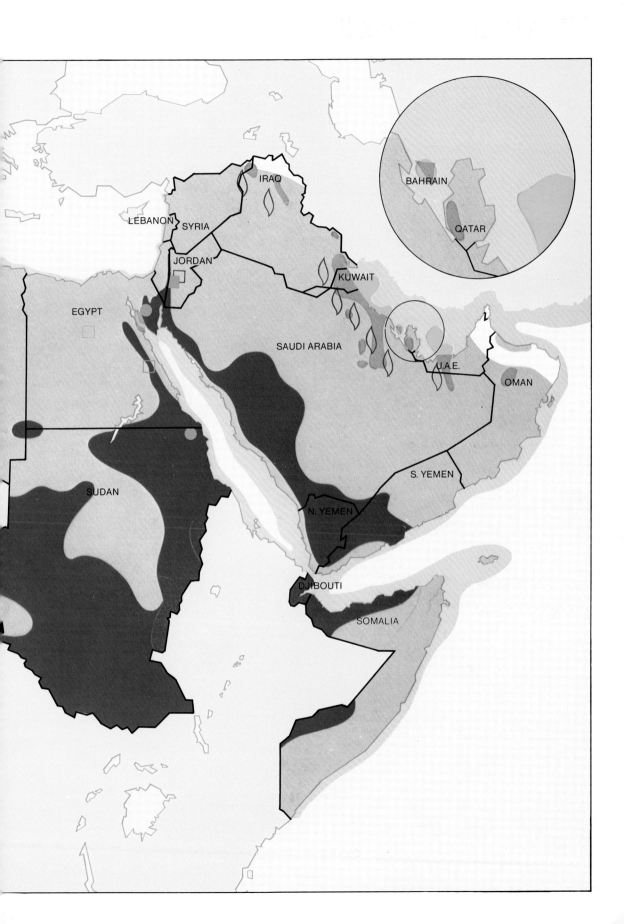

BAHRAIN

QATAR

IRAQ

LEBANON

SYRIA

JORDAN

KUWAIT

EGYPT

SAUDI ARABIA

U.A.E.

OMAN

SUDAN

S. YEMEN

N. YEMEN

DJIBOUTI

SOMALIA

18 Oil Production

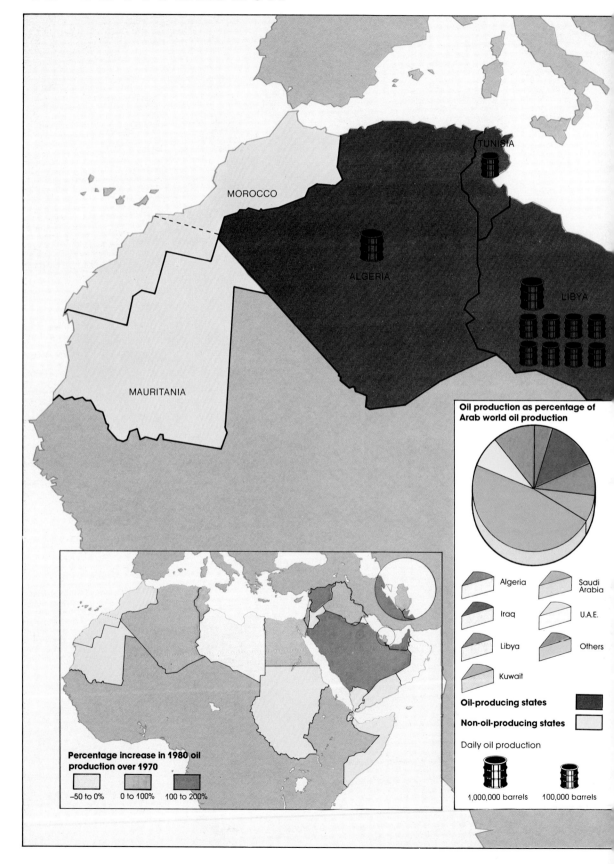

MOROCCO

TUNISIA

ALGERIA

LIBYA

MAURITANIA

Oil production as percentage of Arab world oil production

Algeria

Saudi Arabia

Iraq

U.A.E.

Libya

Others

Kuwait

Oil-producing states

Non-oil-producing states

Daily oil production

1,000,000 barrels   100,000 barrels

Percentage increase in 1980 oil production over 1970

−50 to 0%   0 to 100%   100 to 200%

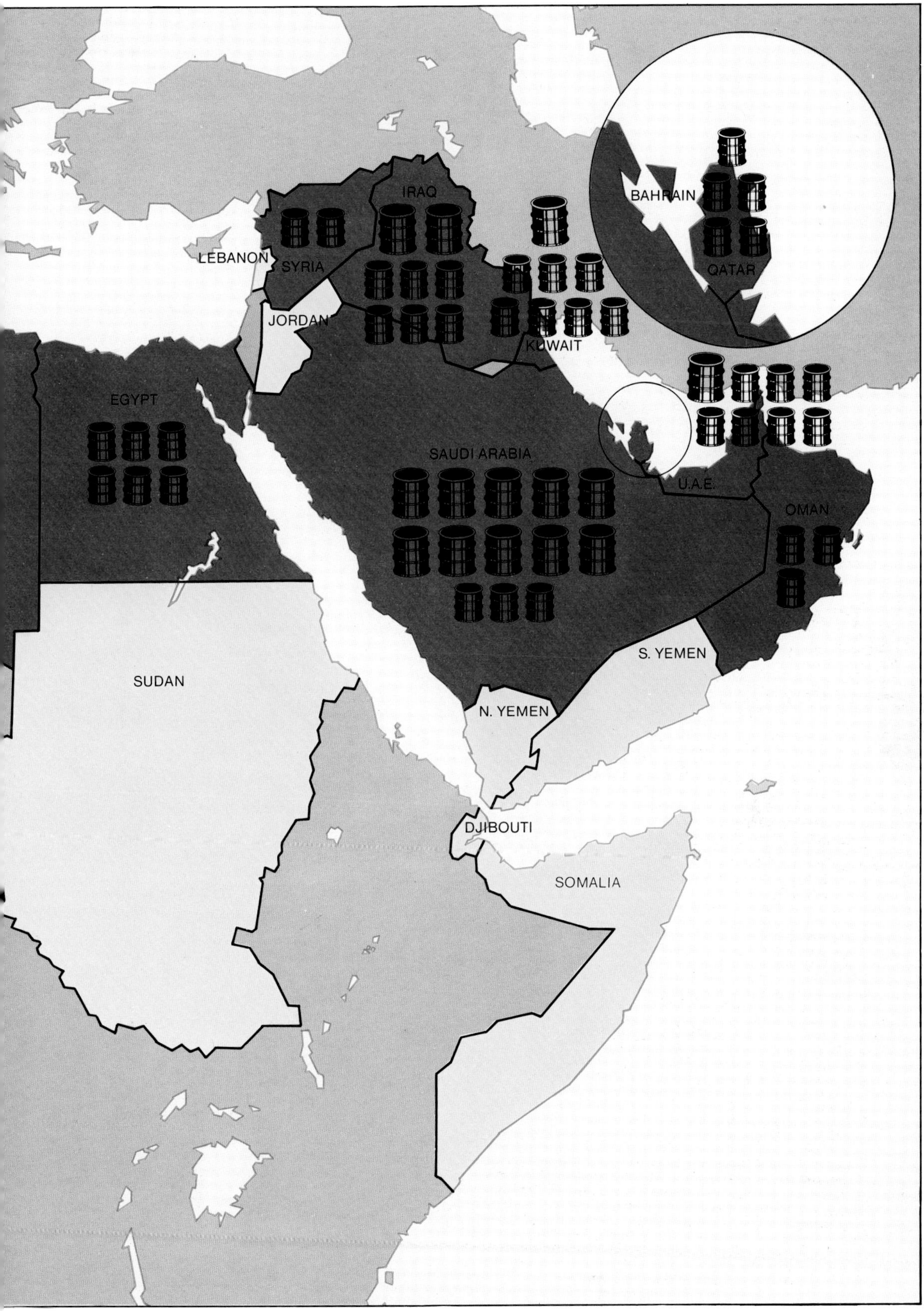
BAHRAIN
QATAR
IRAQ
LEBANON
SYRIA
JORDAN
KUWAIT
EGYPT
SAUDI ARABIA
U.A.E.
OMAN
S. YEMEN
SUDAN
N. YEMEN
DJIBOUTI
SOMALIA

19 The Movement of Oil

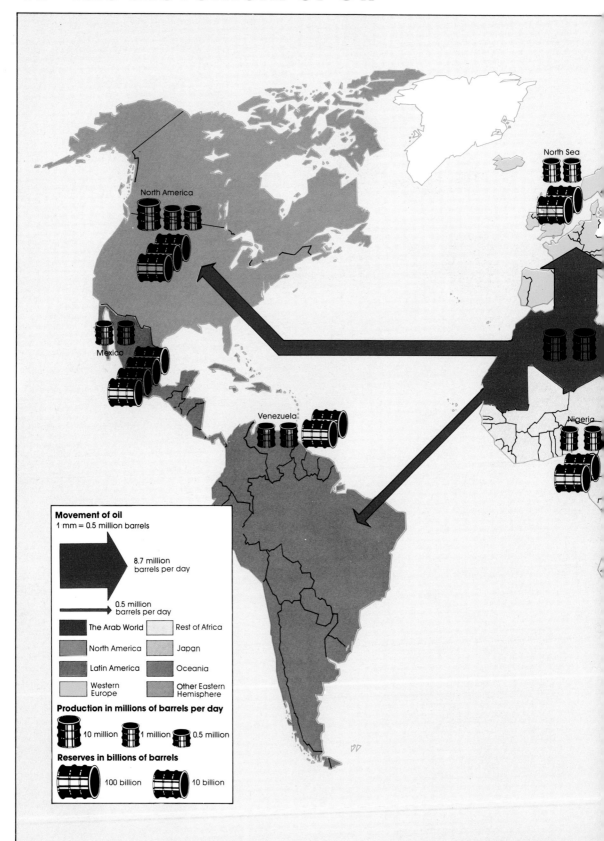

North Sea

North America

Mexico

Venezuela

Nigeria

Movement of oil
1 mm = 0.5 million barrels

8.7 million
barrels per day

0.5 million
barrels per day

The Arab World	Rest of Africa
North America	Japan
Latin America	Oceania
Western Europe	Other Eastern Hemisphere

Production in millions of barrels per day

10 million   1 million   0.5 million

Reserves in billions of barrels

100 billion   10 billion

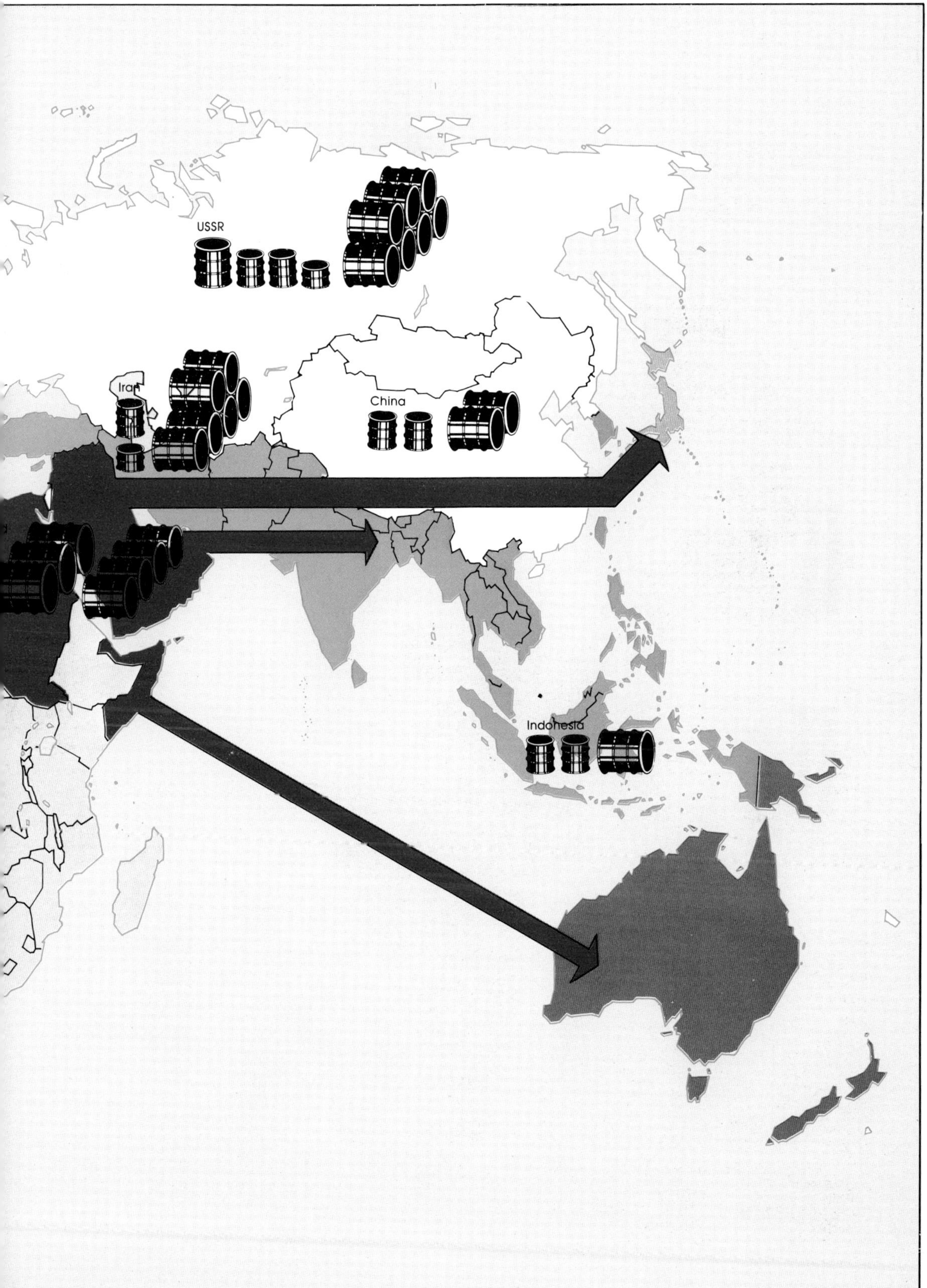

USSR
Iran
China
Indonesia

20 Energy Consumption

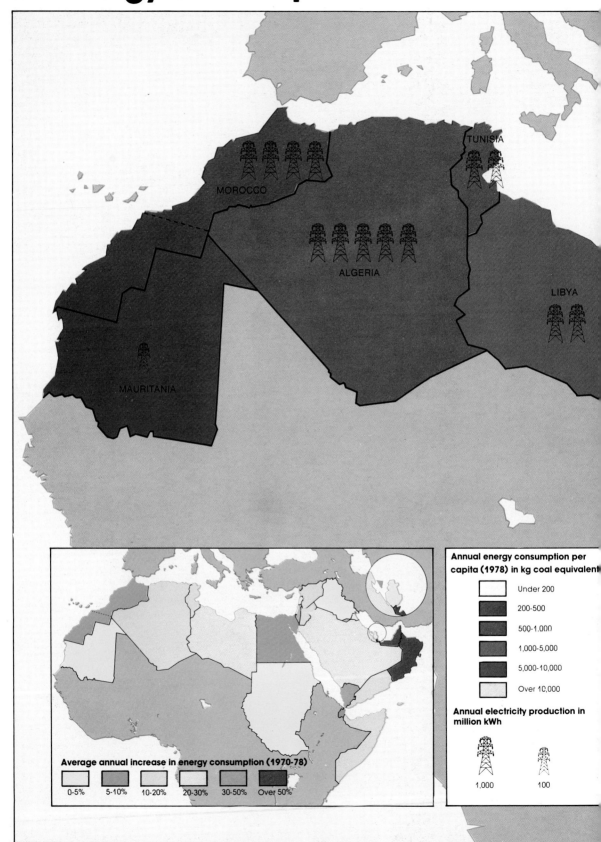

MOROCCO

TUNISIA

ALGERIA

LIBYA

MAURITANIA

Average annual increase in energy consumption (1970-78)

| 0-5% | 5-10% | 10-20% | 20-30% | 30-50% | Over 50% |

Annual energy consumption per capita (1978) in kg coal equivalent

Under 200

200-500

500-1,000

1,000-5,000

5,000-10,000

Over 10,000

Annual electricity production in million kWh

1,000   100

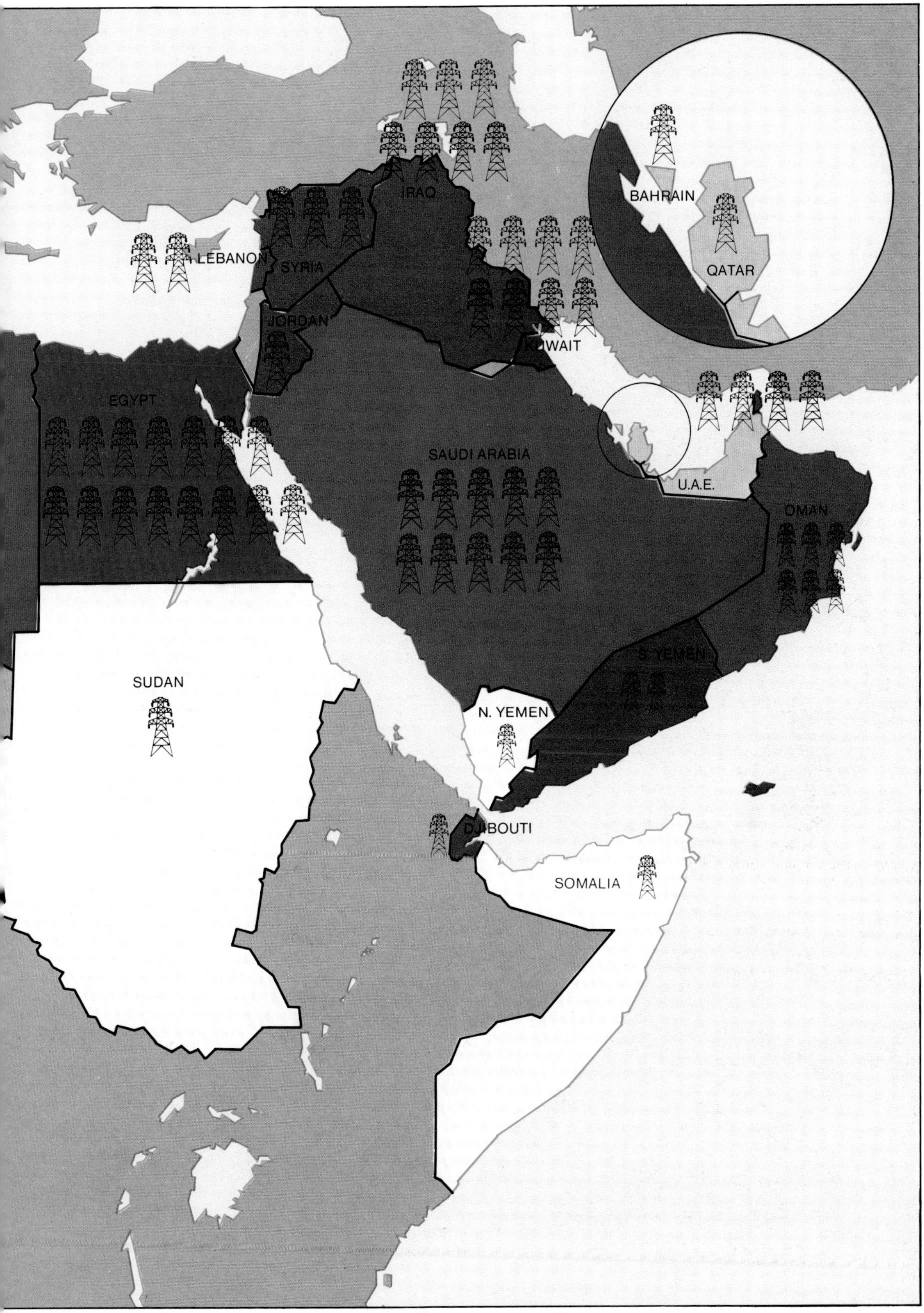

IRAQ
BAHRAIN
QATAR
LEBANON
SYRIA
JORDAN
KUWAIT
EGYPT
SAUDI ARABIA
U.A.E.
OMAN
S. YEMEN
SUDAN
N. YEMEN
DJIBOUTI
SOMALIA

21 Industry and Manufacturing

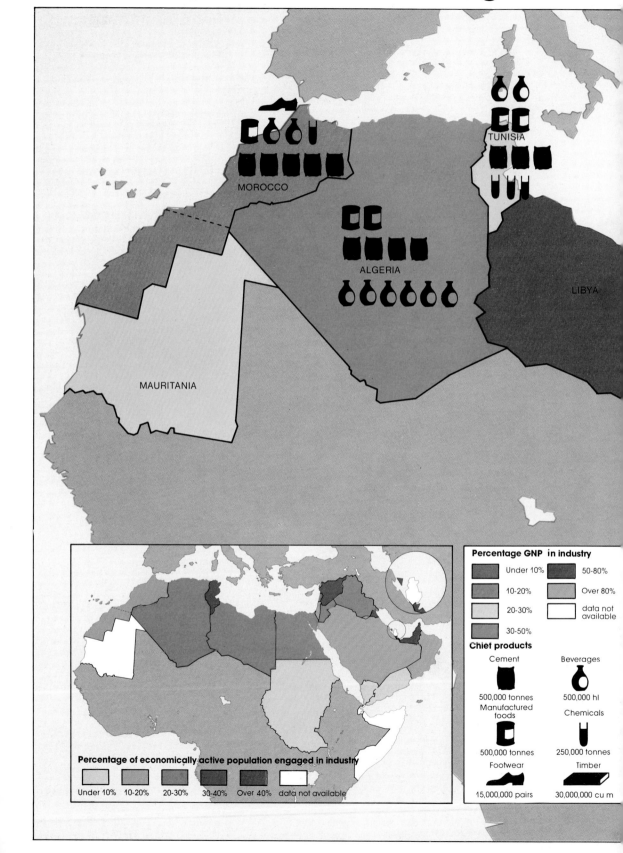

MOROCCO

TUNISIA

ALGERIA

LIBYA

MAURITANIA

Percentage GNP in industry

Under 10%		50-80%	
10-20%		Over 80%	
20-30%		data not available	
30-50%			

Chiet products

Cement
500,000 tonnes

Beverages
500,000 hl

Manufactured foods
500,000 tonnes

Chemicals
250,000 tonnes

Footwear
15,000,000 pairs

Timber
30,000,000 cu m

Percentage of economically active population engaged in industry

Under 10%	10-20%	20-30%	30-40%	Over 40%	data not available

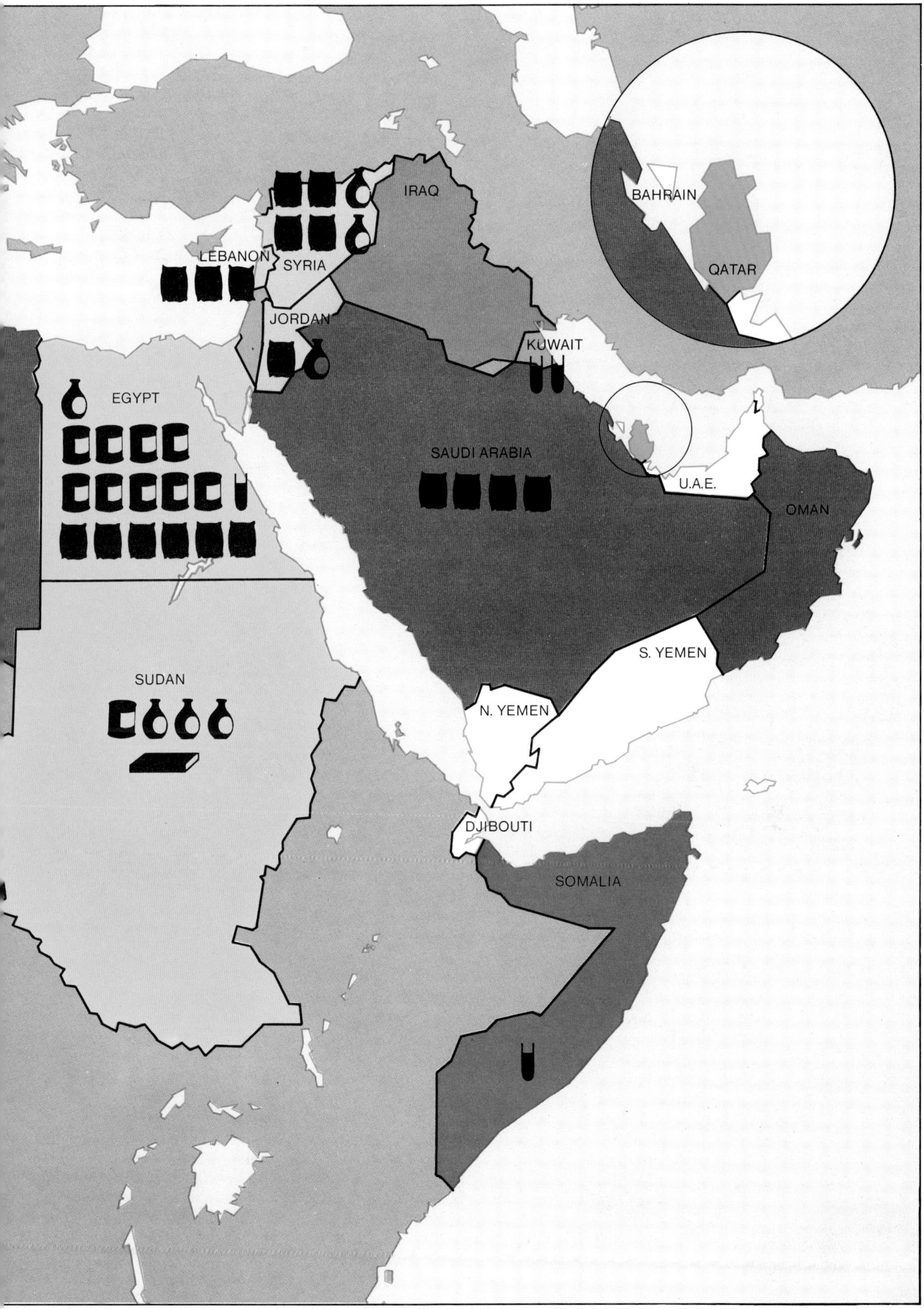

IRAQ
BAHRAIN
QATAR
LEBANON
SYRIA
JORDAN
KUWAIT
EGYPT
SAUDI ARABIA
U.A.E.
OMAN
S. YEMEN
SUDAN
N. YEMEN
DJIBOUTI
SOMALIA

22 Volume of Trade

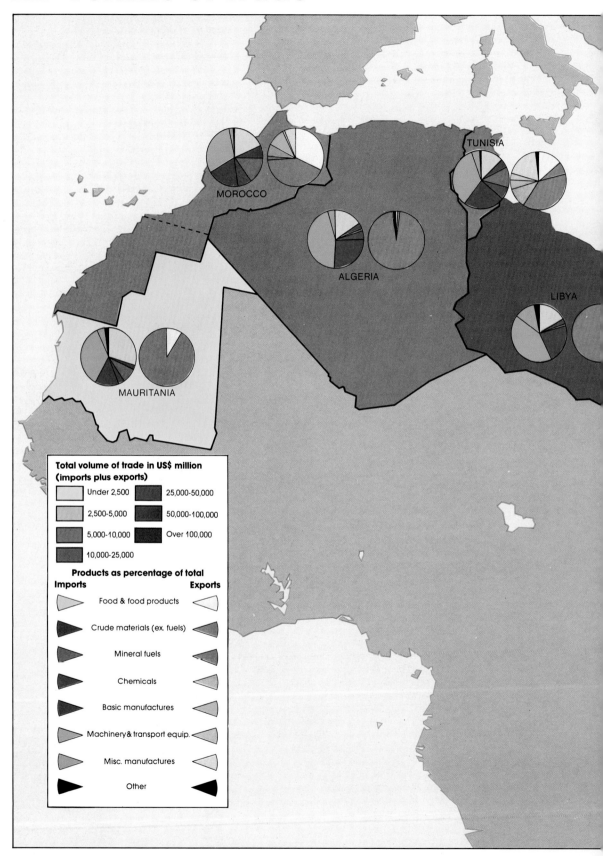

Total volume of trade in US$ million (imports plus exports)

- Under 2,500
- 2,500-5,000
- 5,000-10,000
- 10,000-25,000
- 25,000-50,000
- 50,000-100,000
- Over 100,000

Products as percentage of total

Imports		Exports
	Food & food products	
	Crude materials (ex. fuels)	
	Mineral fuels	
	Chemicals	
	Basic manufactures	
	Machinery & transport equip.	
	Misc. manufactures	
	Other	

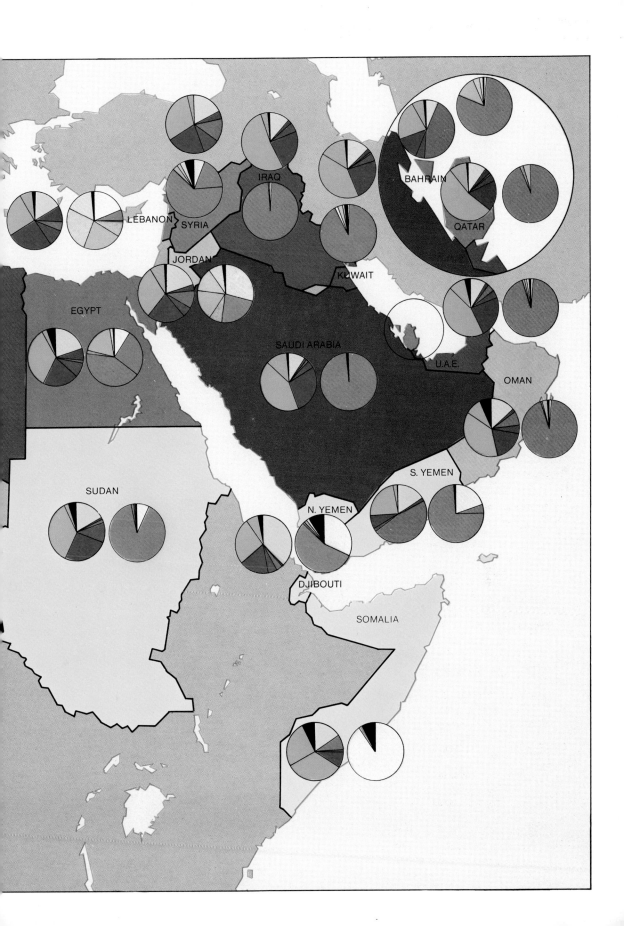

LEBANON

SYRIA

IRAQ

BAHRAIN

QATAR

JORDAN

KUWAIT

EGYPT

SAUDI ARABIA

U.A.E.

OMAN

SUDAN

S. YEMEN

N. YEMEN

DJIBOUTI

SOMALIA

23 Trading Partners

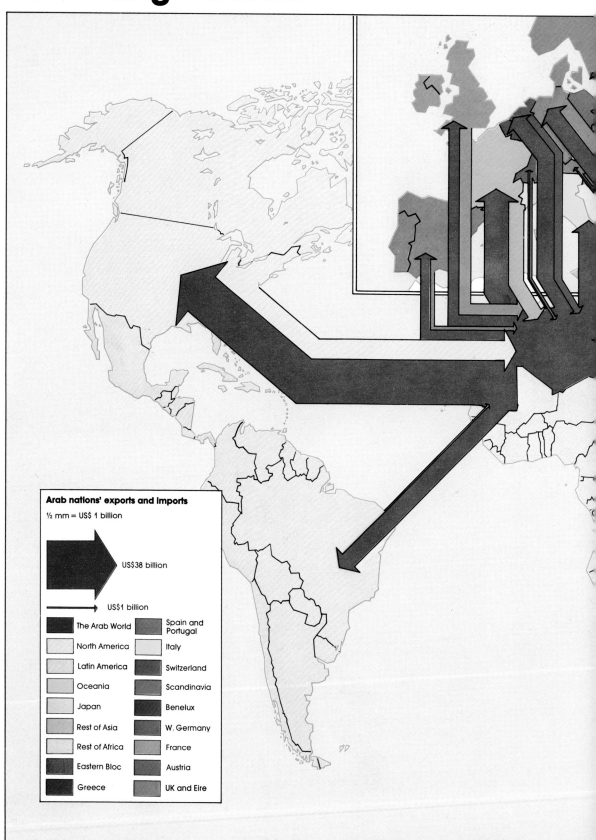

Arab nations' exports and imports

½ mm = US$ 1 billion

US$38 billion

US$1 billion

The Arab World
North America
Latin America
Oceania
Japan
Rest of Asia
Rest of Africa
Eastern Bloc
Greece

Spain and Portugal
Italy
Switzerland
Scandinavia
Benelux
W. Germany
France
Austria
UK and Eire

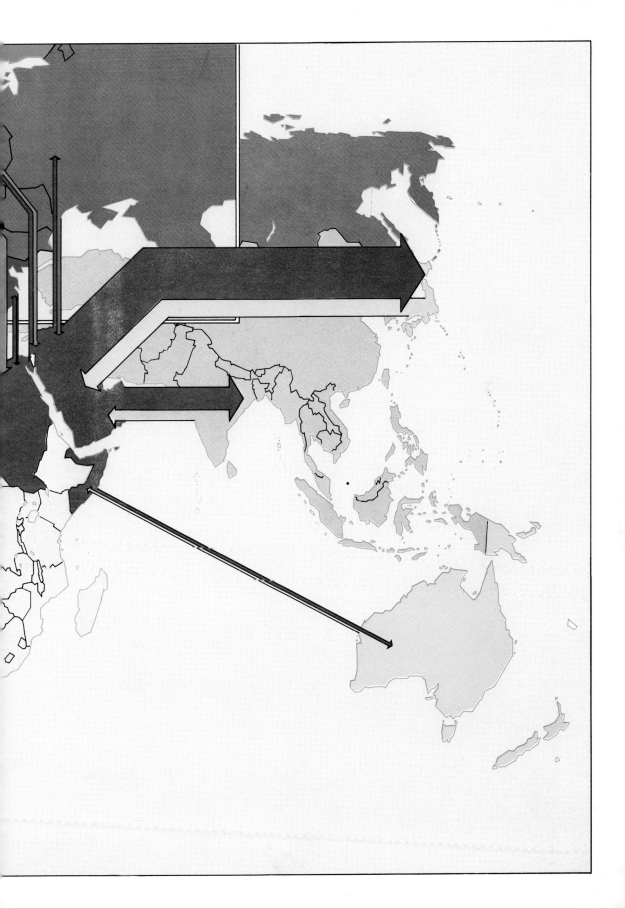

24 National Wealth

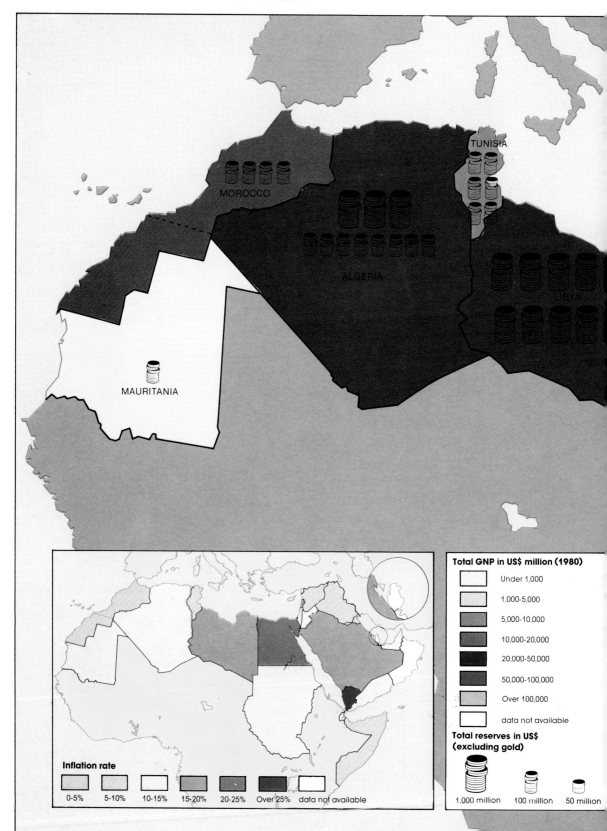

MOROCCO

TUNISIA

ALGERIA

LIBYA

MAURITANIA

Inflation rate

| 0-5% | 5-10% | 10-15% | 15-20% | 20-25% | Over 25% | data not available |

Total GNP in US$ million (1980)

	Under 1,000
	1,000-5,000
	5,000-10,000
	10,000-20,000
	20,000-50,000
	50,000-100,000
	Over 100,000
	data not available

Total reserves in US$ (excluding gold)

1,000 million   100 million   50 million

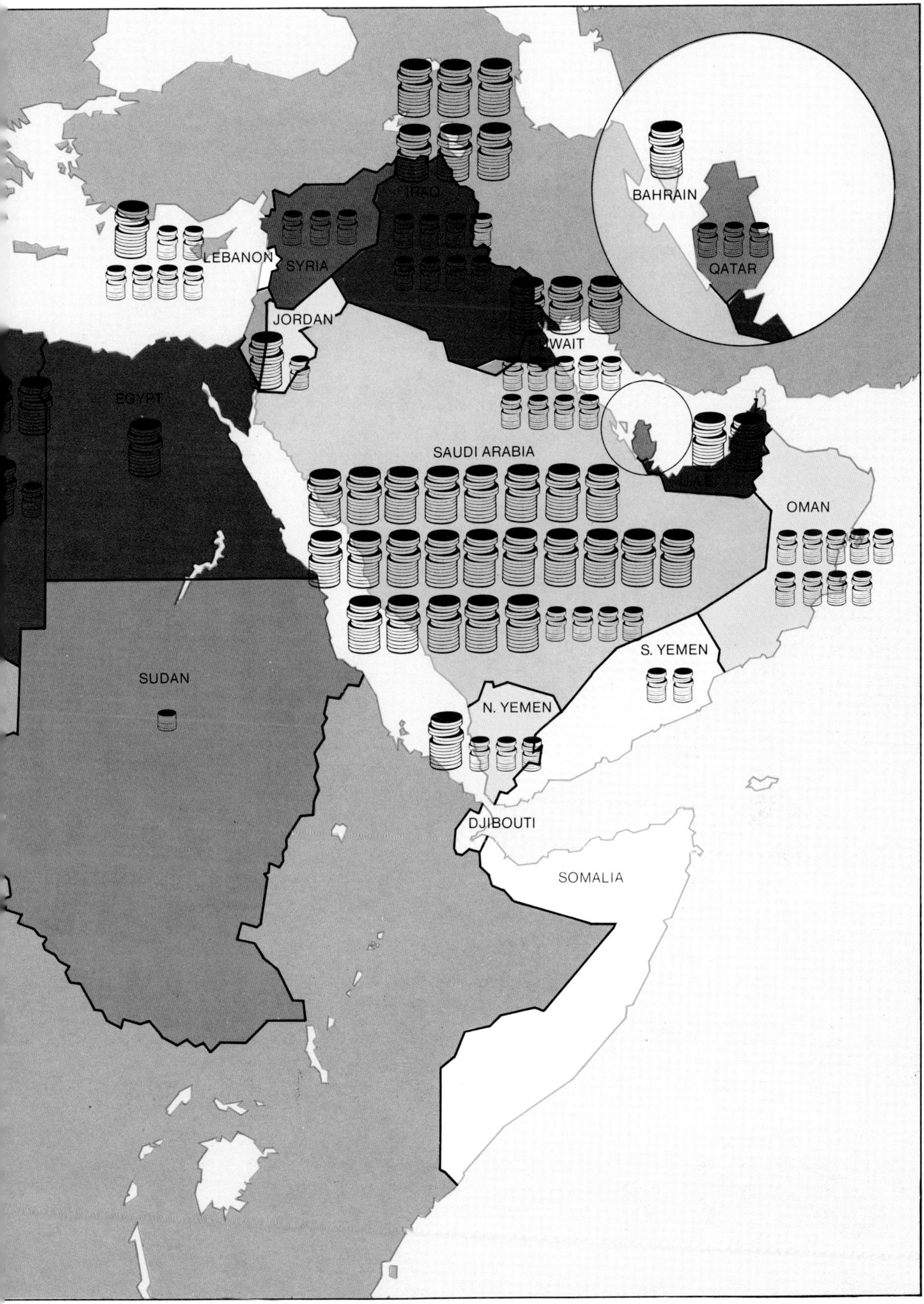

LEBANON
SYRIA
IRAQ
JORDAN
KUWAIT
EGYPT
SAUDI ARABIA
BAHRAIN
QATAR
UAE
OMAN
S. YEMEN
N. YEMEN
SUDAN
DJIBOUTI
SOMALIA

25 Wealth of the Arab World

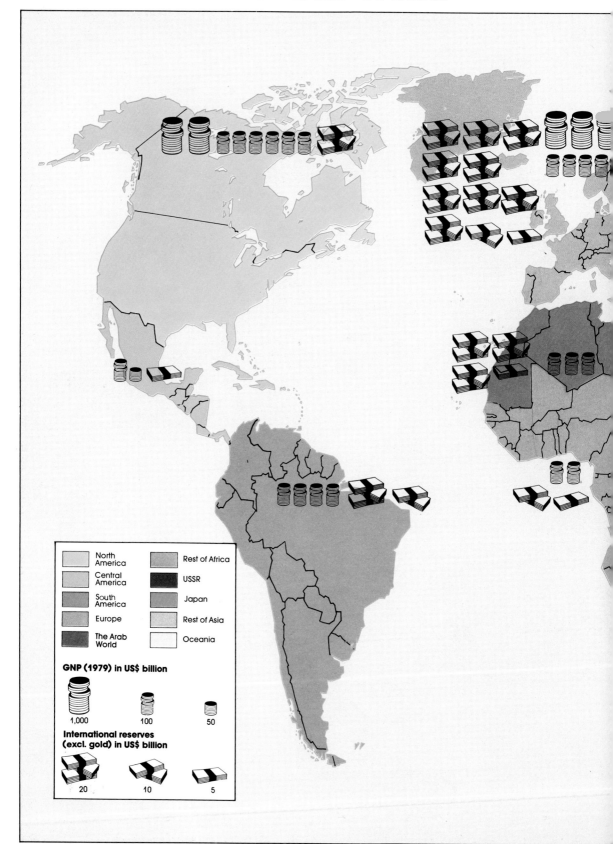

North America

Central America

South America

Europe

The Arab World

Rest of Africa

USSR

Japan

Rest of Asia

Oceania

GNP (1979) in US$ billion

1,000   100   50

International reserves (excl. gold) in US$ billion

20   10   5

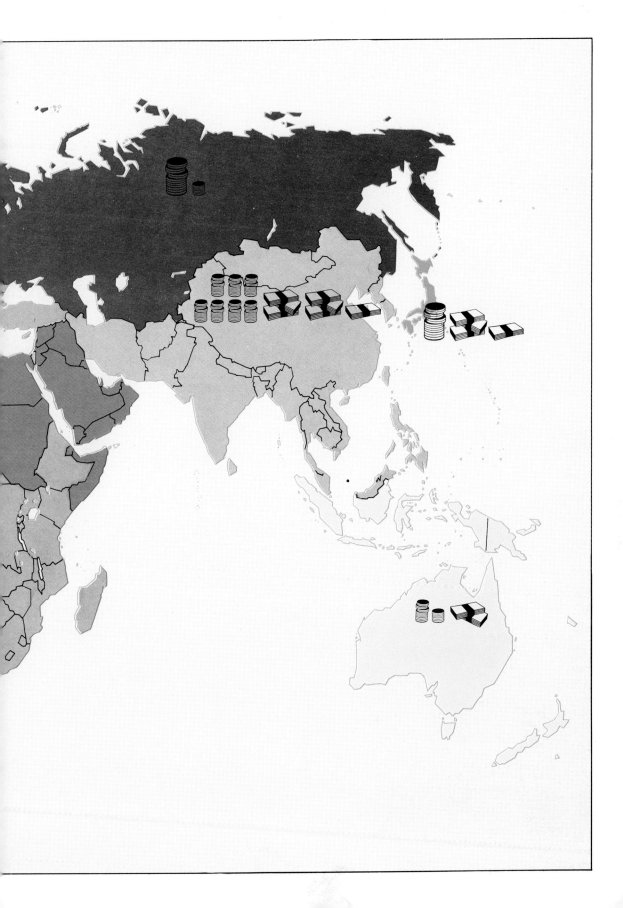

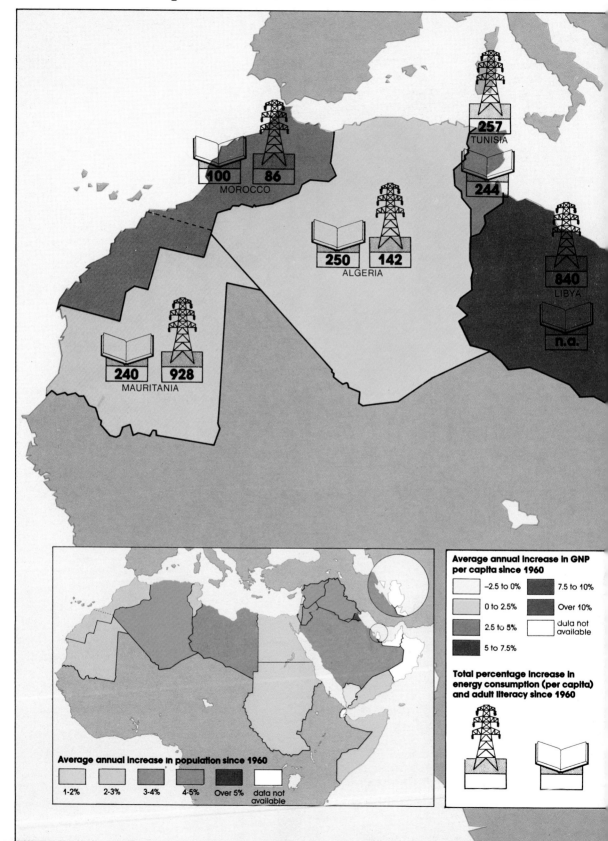

TUNISIA 257 — 244

MOROCCO 100 — 86

ALGERIA 250 — 142

LIBYA 840 — n.a.

MAURITANIA 240 — 928

Average annual increase in GNP per capita since 1960

−2.5 to 0%	7.5 to 10%
0 to 2.5%	Over 10%
2.5 to 5%	data not available
5 to 7.5%	

Total percentage increase in energy consumption (per capita) and adult literacy since 1960

Average annual increase in population since 1960

1-2%	2-3%	3-4%	4-5%	Over 5%	data not available

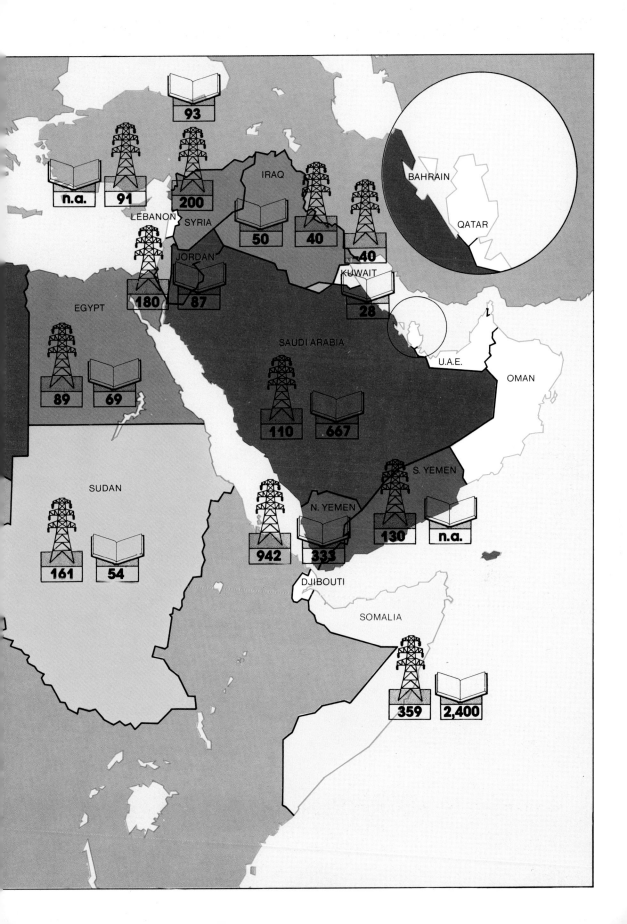

93

n.a. 91 200

IRAQ

BAHRAIN

QATAR

50 40

LEBANON

SYRIA

JORDAN

KUWAIT

40

180 87

28

EGYPT

SAUDI ARABIA

U.A.E.

OMAN

89 69

110 667

S. YEMEN

SUDAN

N. YEMEN

130 n.a.

161 54

942 333

DJIBOUTI

SOMALIA

359 2,400

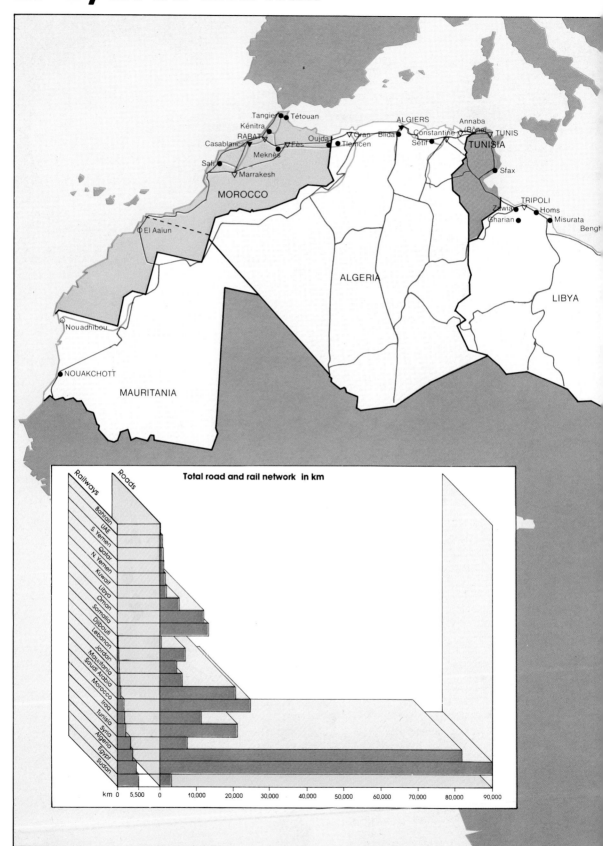

Total road and rail network in km

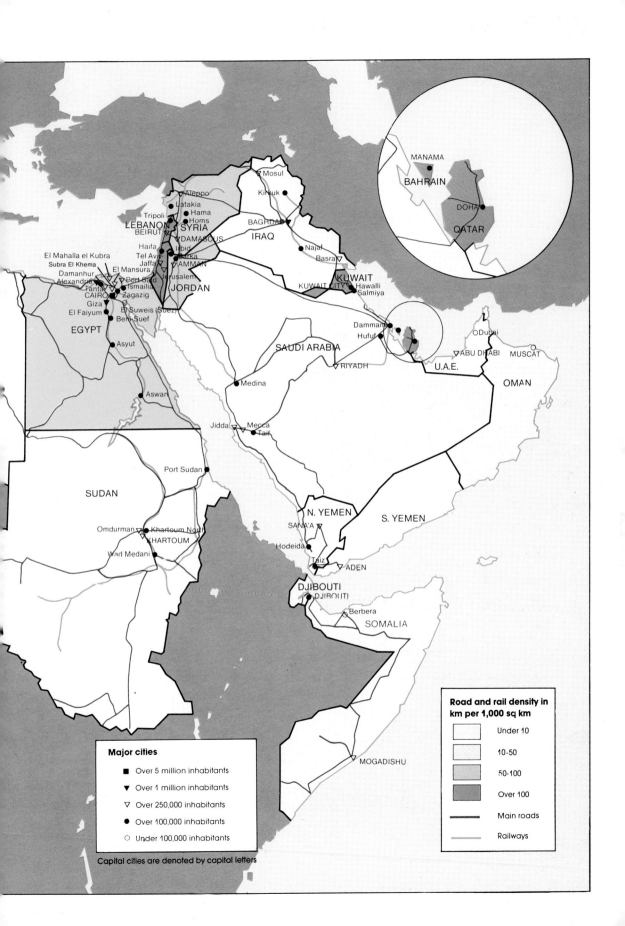

Major cities

■ Over 5 million inhabitants
▼ Over 1 million inhabitants
▽ Over 250,000 inhabitants
● Over 100,000 inhabitants
○ Under 100,000 inhabitants

Capital cities are denoted by capital letters

Road and rail density in km per 1,000 sq km

	Under 10
	10-50
	50-100
	Over 100

Main roads

Railways

28 By Sea and Air

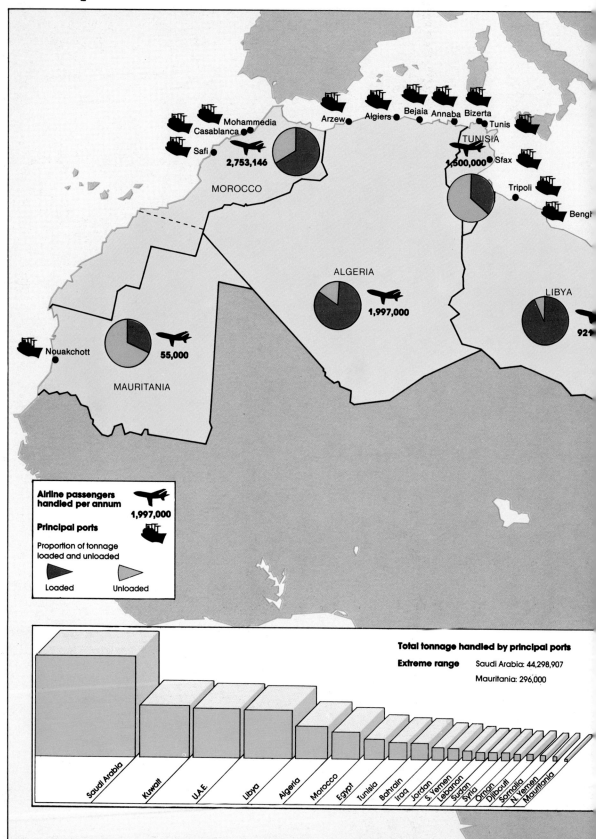

Mohammedia
Casablanca
Safi
Arzew
Algiers
Bejaia
Annaba
Bizerta
Tunis

2,753,146

MOROCCO

TUNISIA

1,500,000

Sfax

Tripoli

Bengl

ALGERIA

1,997,000

LIBYA

921

Nouakchott

55,000

MAURITANIA

Airline passengers
handled per annum

1,997,000

Principal ports

Proportion of tonnage
loaded and unloaded

Loaded   Unloaded

Total tonnage handled by principal ports

Extreme range   Saudi Arabia: 44,298,907

Mauritania: 296,000

Saudi Arabia
Kuwait
U.A.E.
Libya
Algeria
Morocco
Egypt
Tunisia
Bahrain
Iraq
Jordan
S. Yemen
Lebanon
Sudan
Syria
Oman
Djibouti
Somalia
N. Yemen
Mauritania

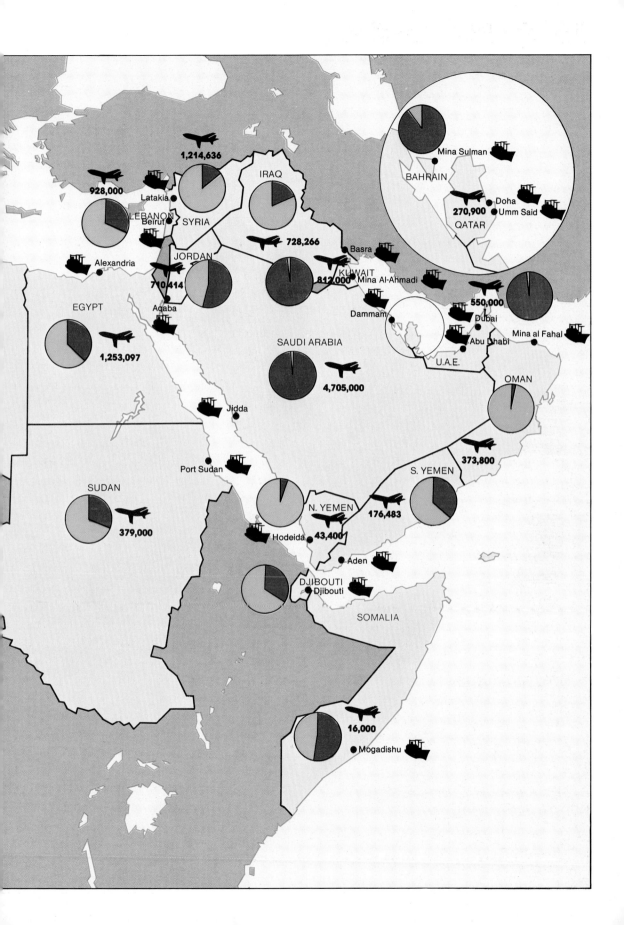

BAHRAIN

Mina Sulman

270,900 Doha
Umm Said

QATAR

1,214,636

928,000

Latakia

IRAQ

LEBANON
Beirut

SYRIA

JORDAN

Alexandria

728,266

Basra

KUWAIT
812,000 Mina Al-Ahmadi

550,000 Dubai
Abu Dhabi Mina al Fahal

710,414

Aqaba

EGYPT

Dammam

U.A.E.

1,253,097

SAUDI ARABIA

OMAN

Jidda

4,705,000

Port Sudan

S. YEMEN

373,800

SUDAN

N. YEMEN

176,483

379,000

Hodeida 43,400

Aden

DJIBOUTI
Djibouti

SOMALIA

16,000

Mogadishu

29 The Media

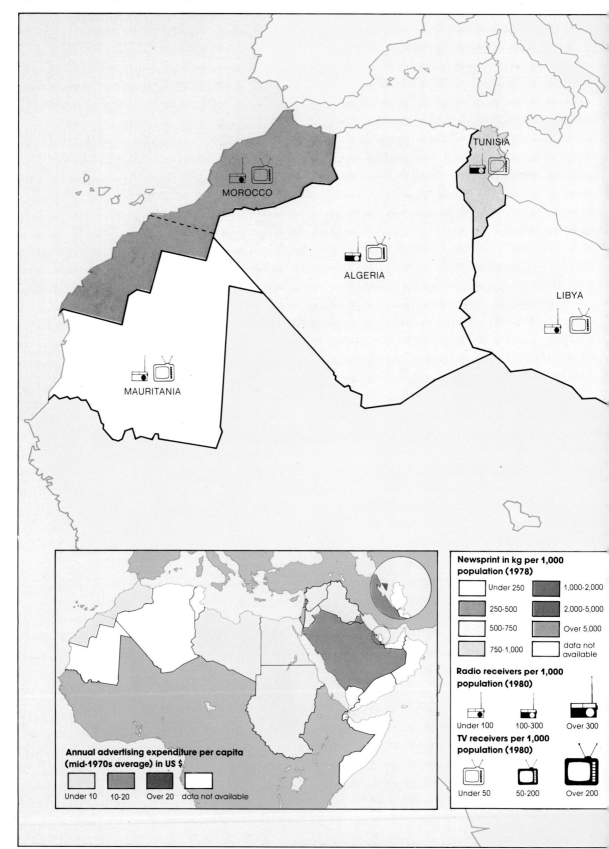

MOROCCO

TUNISIA

ALGERIA

LIBYA

MAURITANIA

Newsprint in kg per 1,000 population (1978)

Under 250	1,000-2,000
250-500	2,000-5,000
500-750	Over 5,000
750-1,000	data not available

Radio receivers per 1,000 population (1980)

Under 100	100-300	Over 300

TV receivers per 1,000 population (1980)

Under 50	50-200	Over 200

Annual advertising expenditure per capita (mid-1970s average) in US $

Under 10	10-20	Over 20	data not available

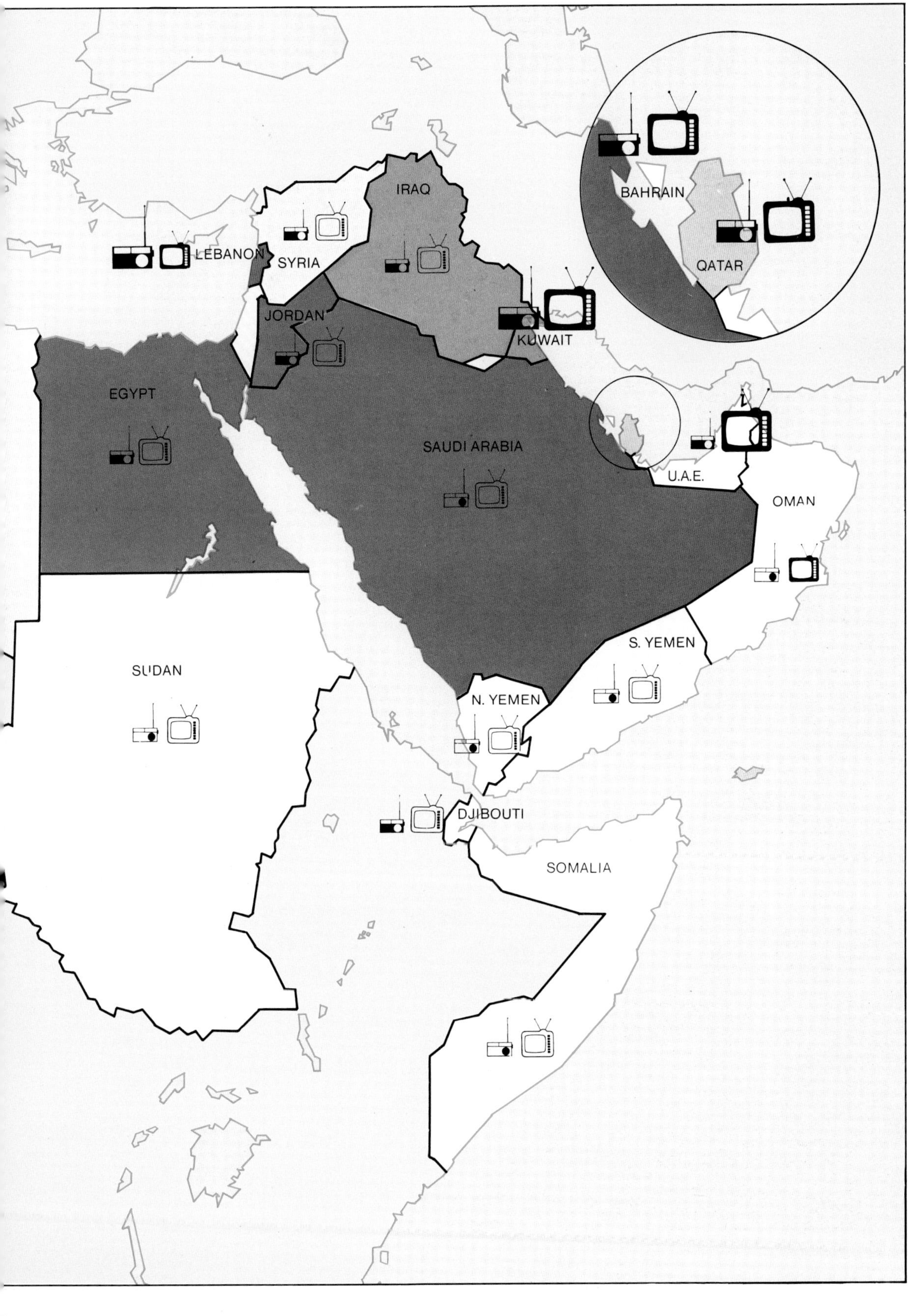
IRAQ
LEBANON
SYRIA
JORDAN
KUWAIT
BAHRAIN
QATAR
EGYPT
SAUDI ARABIA
U.A.E.
OMAN
S. YEMEN
SUDAN
N. YEMEN
DJIBOUTI
SOMALIA

30 Government and Politics

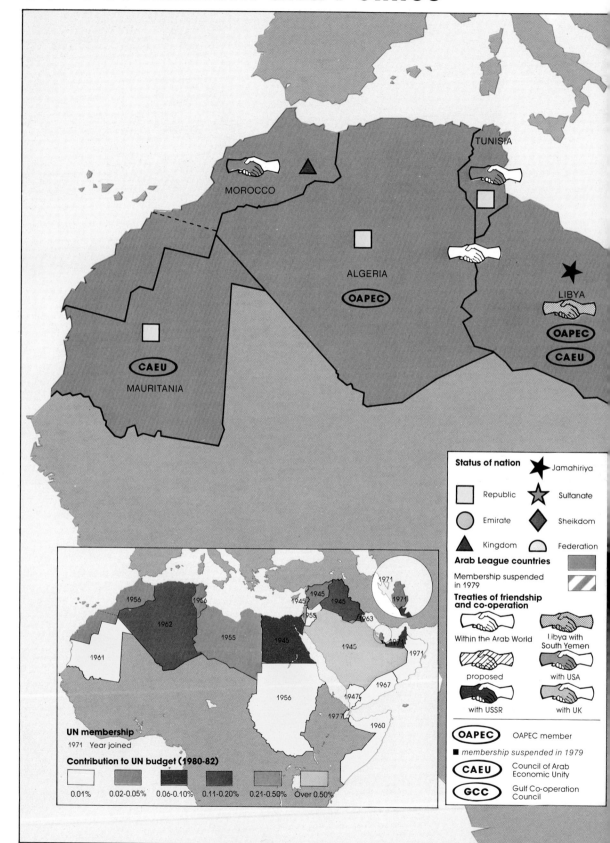

TUNISIA

MOROCCO

ALGERIA

OAPEC

LIBYA

OAPEC

CAEU

CAEU

MAURITANIA

Status of nation

Jamahiriya

Republic   Sultanate

Emirate   Sheikdom

Kingdom   Federation

Arab League countries

Membership suspended
in 1979

**Treaties of friendship
and co-operation**

Within the Arab World   Libya with
South Yemen

proposed   with USA

with USSR   with UK

OAPEC OAPEC member

■ *membership suspended in 1979*

CAEU Council of Arab
Economic Unity

GCC Gulf Co-operation
Council

1956   1956   1945   1945   1945   1971   1971
1962   1955   1945   1963
1955   1945   1971   1971
1961   1945
1956   1967
1947
1977   1960

UN membership

1971   Year joined

Contribution to UN budget (1980-82)

0.01%   0.02-0.05%   0.06-0.10%   0.11-0.20%   0.21-0.50%   Over 0.50%

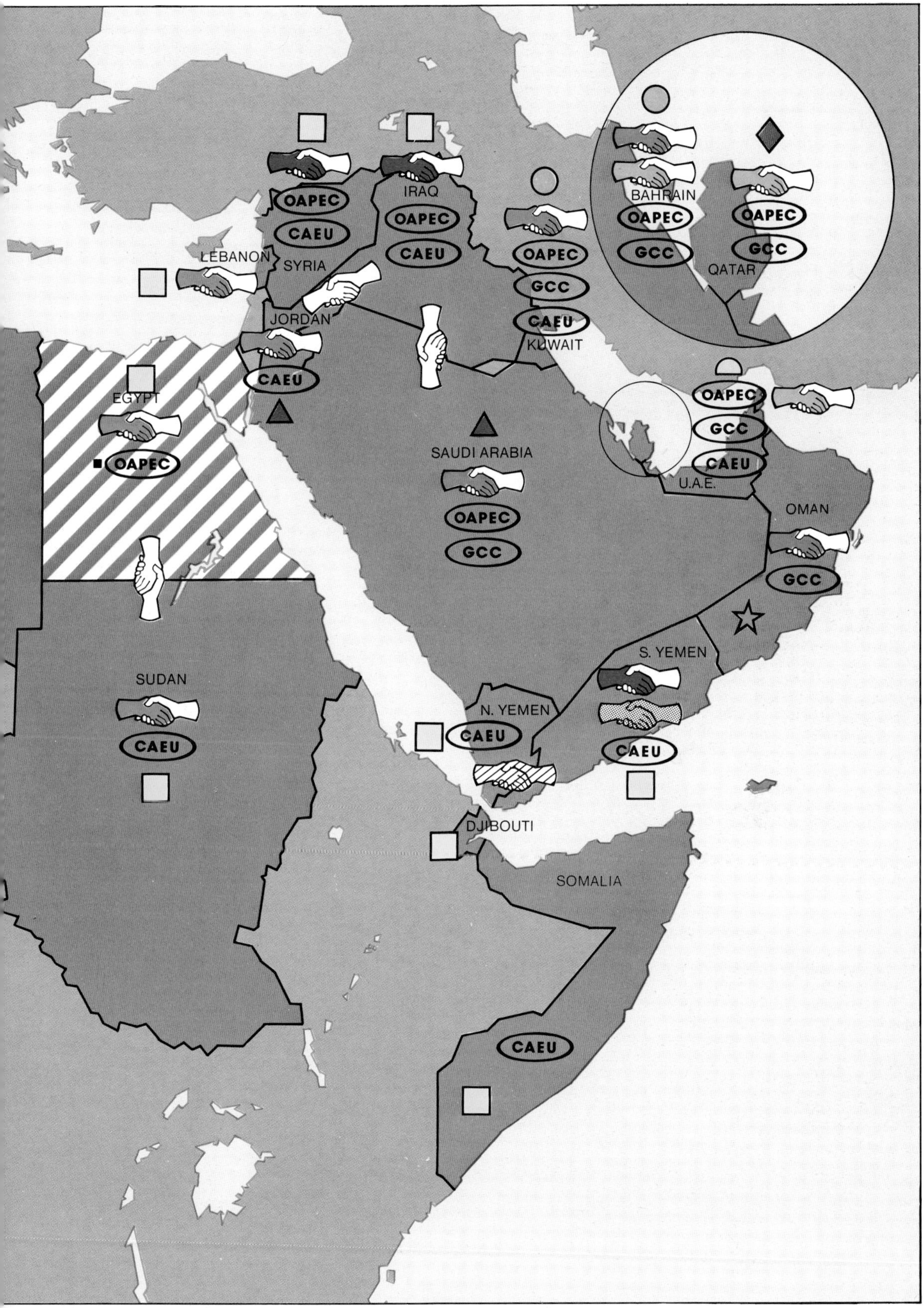

IRAQ
OAPEC
CAEU
OAPEC
CAEU
LEBANON
SYRIA
JORDAN
CAEU
OAPEC
GCC
CAEU
KUWAIT
BAHRAIN
OAPEC
GCC
OAPEC
GCC
QATAR
EGYPT
OAPEC
SAUDI ARABIA
OAPEC
GCC
OAPEC
GCC
CAEU
U.A.E.
OMAN
GCC
S. YEMEN
CAEU
N. YEMEN
CAEU
SUDAN
CAEU
DJIBOUTI
SOMALIA
CAEU

31 Military Expenditure

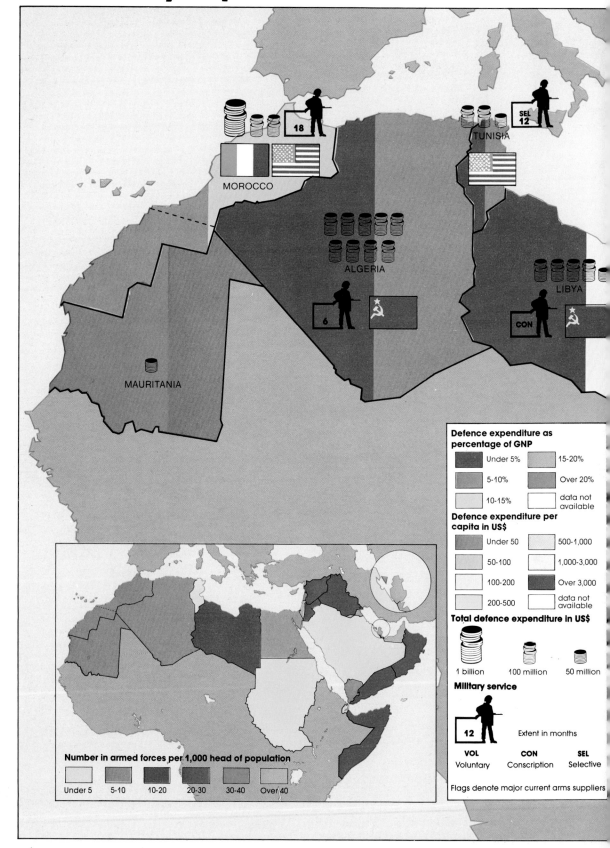

MOROCCO

18

TUNISIA

SEL
12

ALGERIA

6

LIBYA

CON

MAURITANIA

Defence expenditure as percentage of GNP

Under 5%	15-20%
5-10%	Over 20%
10-15%	data not available

Defence expenditure per capita in US$

Under 50	500-1,000
50-100	1,000-3,000
100-200	Over 3,000
200-500	data not available

Total defence expenditure in US$

1 billion   100 million   50 million

Military service

12   Extent in months

VOL
Voluntary

CON
Conscription

SEL
Selective

Flags denote major current arms suppliers

Number in armed forces per 1,000 head of population

| Under 5 | 5-10 | 10-20 | 20-30 | 30-40 | Over 40 |

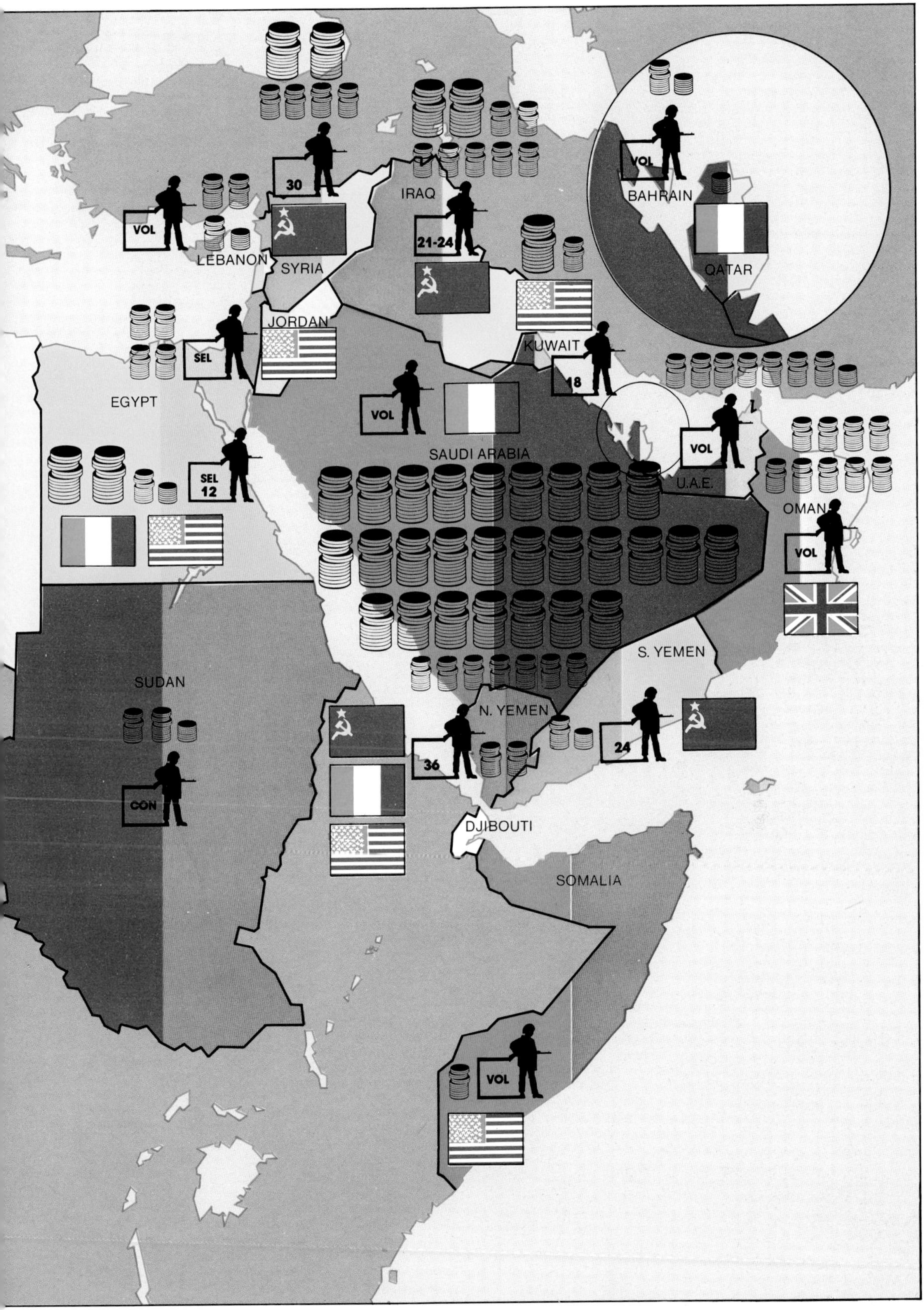

30
VOL
LEBANON
SYRIA
IRAQ
21-24
BAHRAIN
QATAR
VOL
JORDAN
KUWAIT
18
SEL
EGYPT
VOL
SAUDI ARABIA
VOL
U.A.E.
SEL
12
OMAN
VOL
S. YEMEN
SUDAN
N. YEMEN
36
24
CON
DJIBOUTI
SOMALIA
VOL

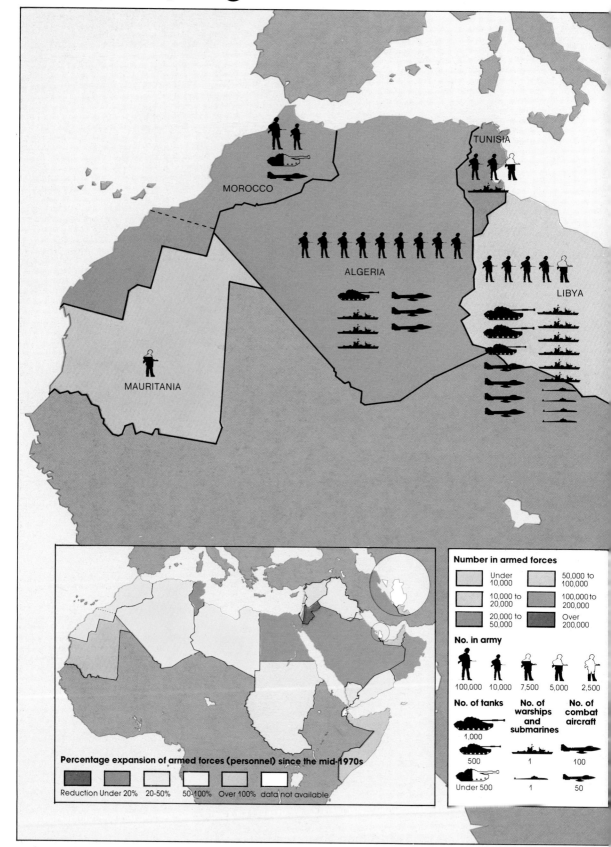

MOROCCO

TUNISIA

ALGERIA

LIBYA

MAURITANIA

Number in armed forces

Under 10,000		50,000 to 100,000	
10,000 to 20,000		100,000 to 200,000	
20,000 to 50,000		Over 200,000	

No. in army

100,000	10,000	7,500	5,000	2,500

No. of tanks	**No. of warships and submarines**	**No. of combat aircraft**
1,000		
500	1	100
Under 500	1	50

Percentage expansion of armed forces (personnel) since the mid-1970s

Reduction	Under 20%	20-50%	50-100%	Over 100%	data not available

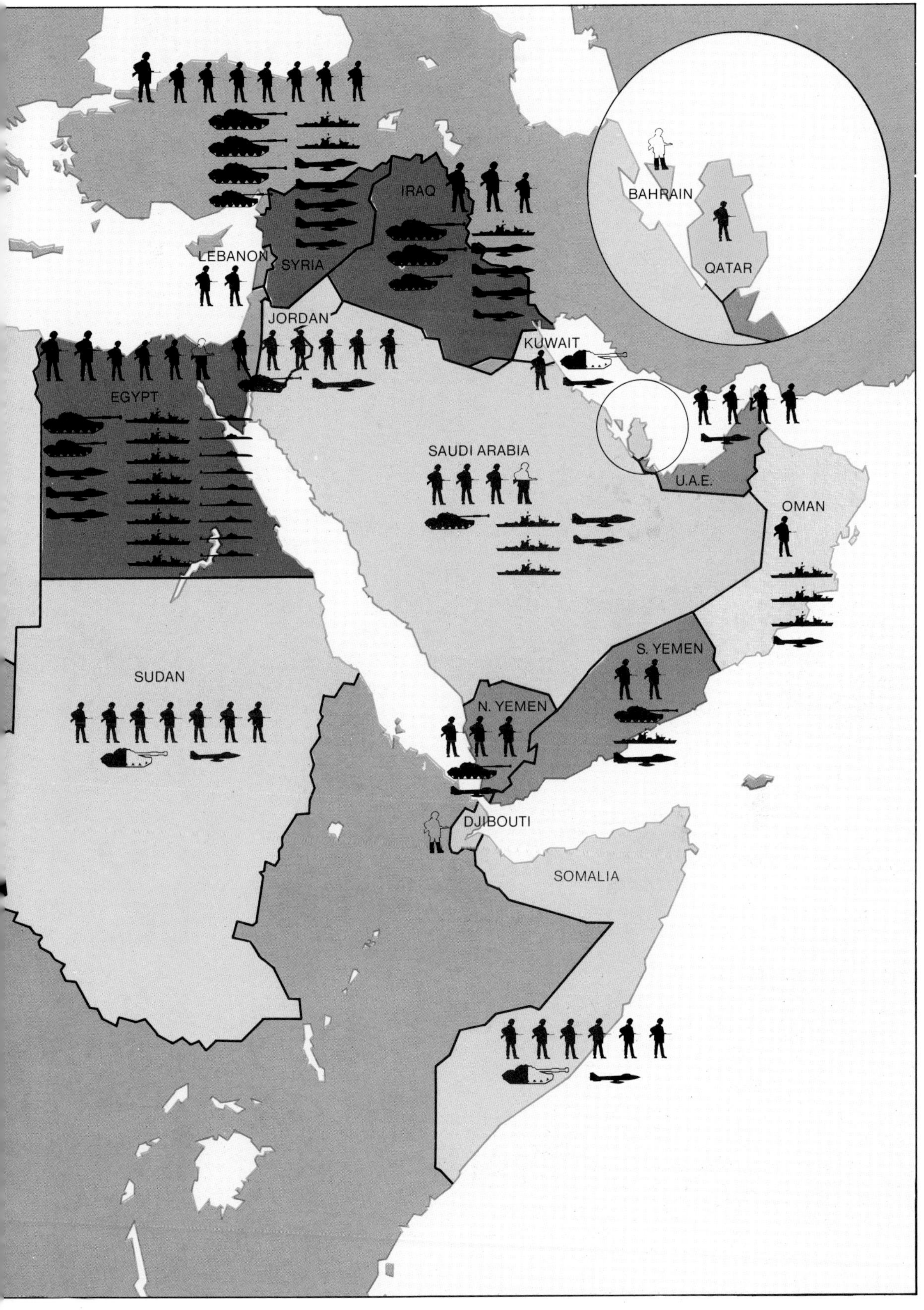

IRAQ
BAHRAIN
QATAR
LEBANON
SYRIA
JORDAN
KUWAIT
EGYPT
SAUDI ARABIA
U.A.E.
OMAN
S. YEMEN
SUDAN
N. YEMEN
DJIBOUTI
SOMALIA

33 Comparative Military Strength

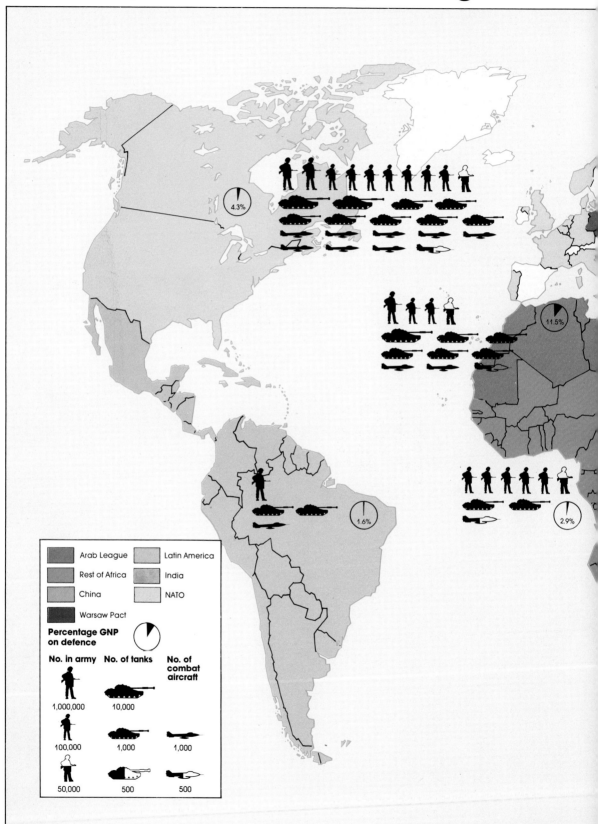

4.3%

11.5%

2.9%

1.6%

Arab League

Rest of Africa

China

Warsaw Pact

Latin America

India

NATO

Percentage GNP on defence

No. in army   No. of tanks   No. of combat aircraft

1,000,000   10,000

100,000   1,000   1,000

50,000   500   500

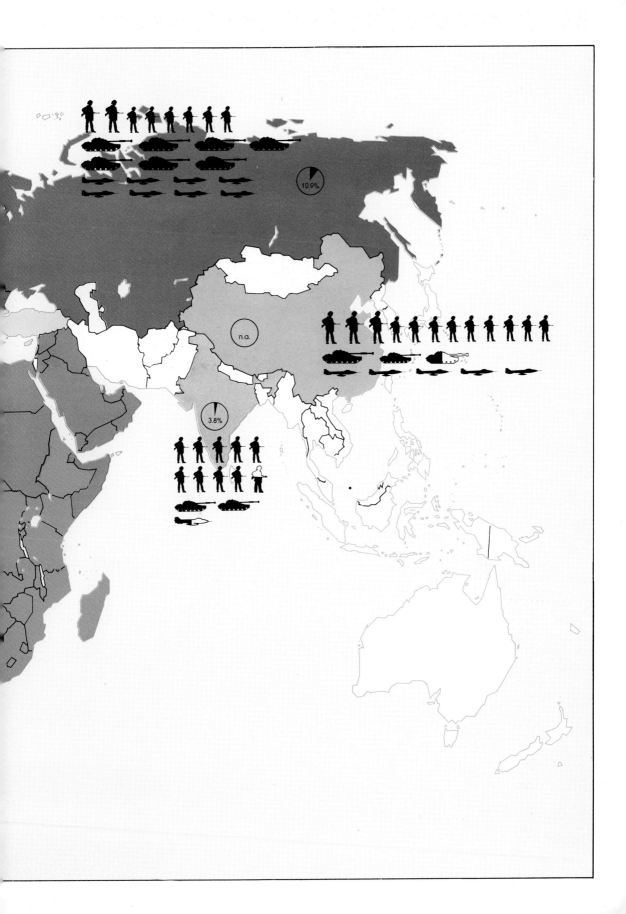

10.9%

n.a.

3.8%

34 Cradles of Civilization

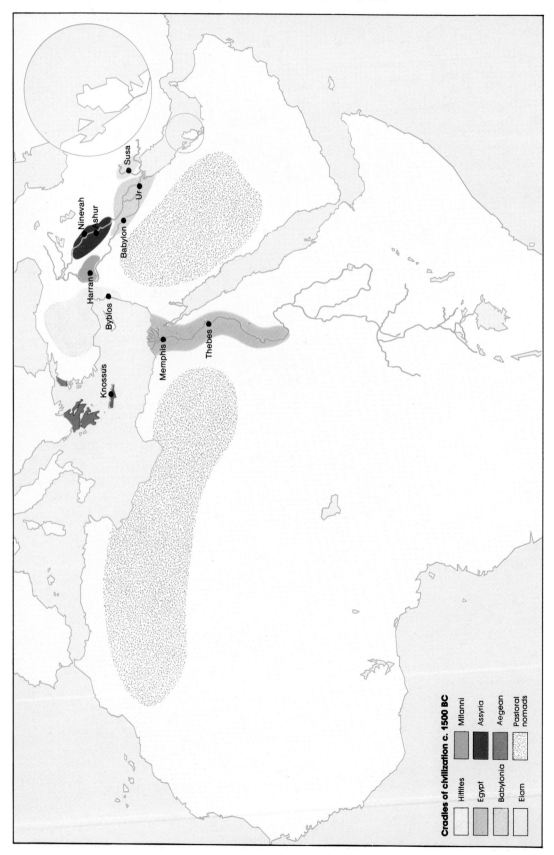

Susa

Ninevah

Ashur

Ur

Babylon

Harran

Byblos

Memphis

Thebes

Knossus

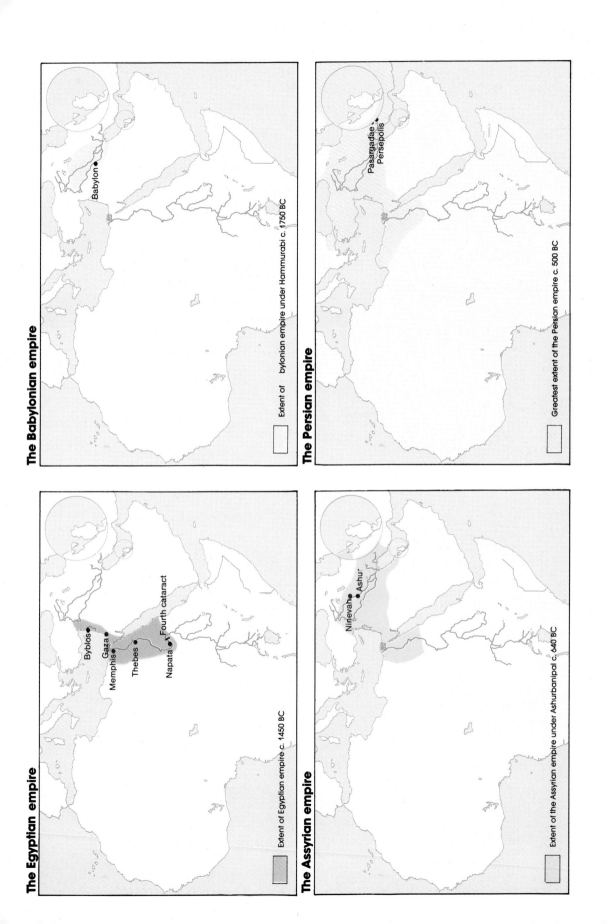

The Egyptian empire

Byblos
Gaza
Memphis
Thebes
Napata
Fourth cataract

Extent of Egyptian empire c. 1450 BC

The Babylonian empire

Babylon

Extent of babylonian empire under Hammurabi c. 1750 BC

The Assyrian empire

Nineveh
Ashur

Extent of the Assyrian empire under Ashurbanipal c. 640 BC

The Persian empire

Pasargadae
Persepolis

Greatest extent of the Persian empire c. 500 BC

35 The Classical Influence

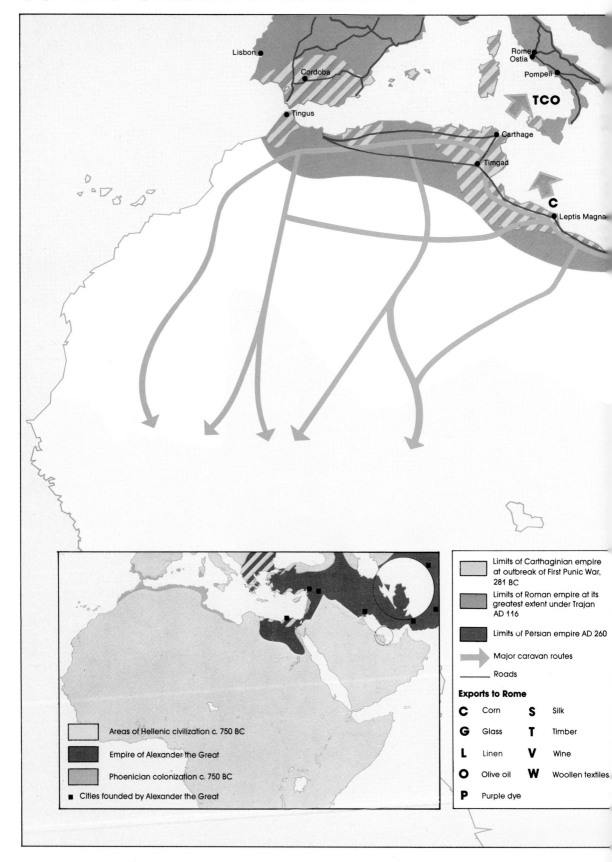

Lisbon

Cordoba

Tingus

Rome
Ostia

Pompeii

TCO

Carthage

Timgad

C

Leptis Magna

Limits of Carthaginian empire
at outbreak of First Punic War,
281 BC

Limits of Roman empire at its
greatest extent under Trajan
AD 116

Limits of Persian empire AD 260

Major caravan routes

Roads

Exports to Rome

C Corn   **S** Silk

G Glass   **T** Timber

L Linen   **V** Wine

O Olive oil   **W** Woollen textiles

P Purple dye

Areas of Hellenic civilization c. 750 BC

Empire of Alexander the Great

Phoenician colonization c. 750 BC

■ Cities founded by Alexander the Great

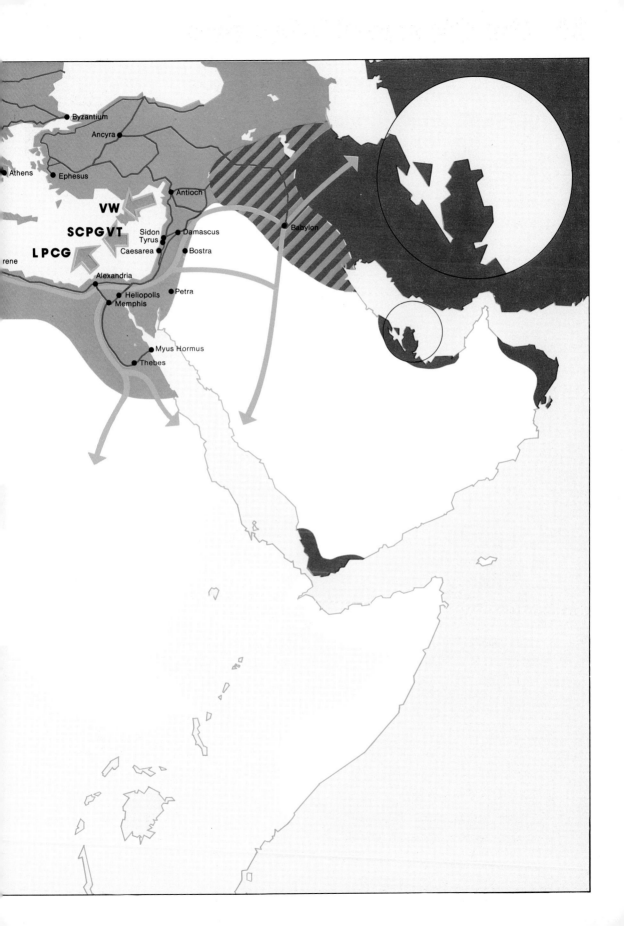

Byzantium

Ancyra

Athens

Ephesus

Antioch

VW

SCPGVT

Sidon
Tyrus

Damascus

LPCG

Caesarea

Bostra

rene

Babylon

Alexandria

Heliopolis

Petra

Memphis

Myus Hormus

Thebes

36 The Expansion of Islam

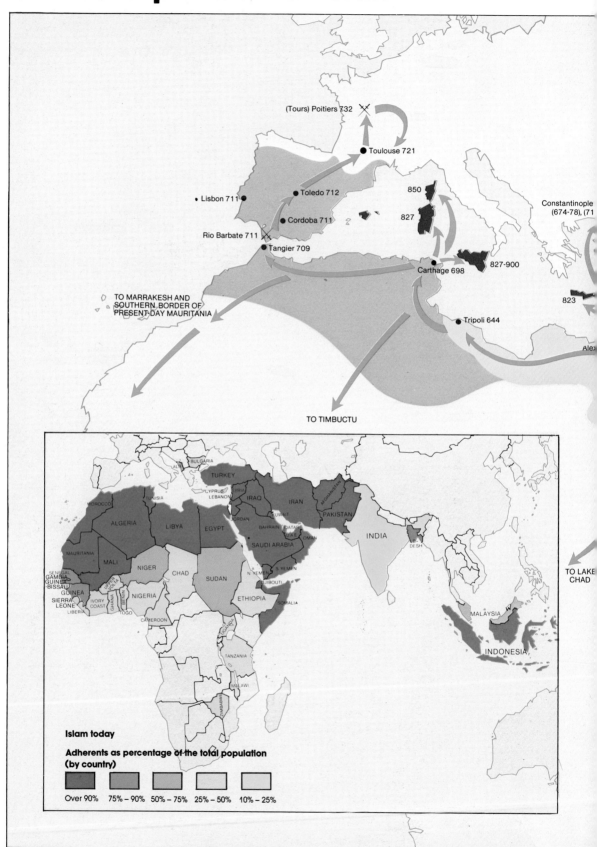

(Tours) Poitiers 732 ✕✕

Toulouse 721

850

827

Toledo 712

• Lisbon 711 •

Cordoba 711 •

Constantinople
(674-78), (71

Rio Barbate 711 ✕

Tangier 709

Carthage 698

827-900

TO MARRAKESH AND
SOUTHERN BORDER OF
PRESENT-DAY MAURITANIA

823

Tripoli 644

Ale

TO TIMBUCTU

BULGARIA

ALB

TURKEY

CYPRUS
LEBANON

SYRIA

IRAQ

IRAN

AFGHANISTAN

MOROCCO

TUNISIA

JORDAN

KUWAIT

PAKISTAN

ALGERIA

LIBYA

EGYPT

BAHRAIN QATAR

U.A.E.

INDIA

SAUDI ARABIA

OMAN

DESH

MAURITANIA

MALI

NIGER

CHAD

SUDAN

N. YEMEN

S. YEMEN

DJIBOUTI

TO LAKE
CHAD

SENEGAL
GAMBIA
GUINEA-
BISSAU

UPPER
VOLTA

GUINEA

SIERRA
LEONE

LIBERIA

IVORY
COAST

GHANA

BENIN

TOGO

NIGERIA

ETHIOPIA

SOMALIA

MALAYSIA

W

CAMEROON

UGANDA

INDONESIA

TANZANIA

MALAWI

ZIMBABWE

Islam today

**Adherents as percentage of the total population
(by country)**

Over 90%   75% – 90%   50% – 75%   25% – 50%   10% – 25%

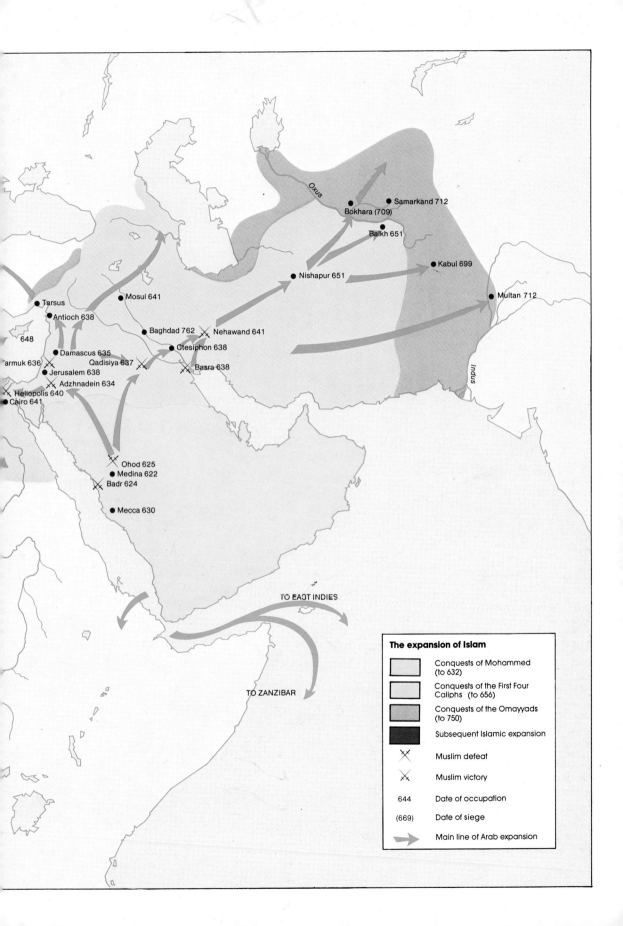

Oxus

● Samarkand 712
Bokhara (709)
● Balkh 651

● Kabul 699

● Multan 712

● Nishapur 651

● Mosul 641

● Tarsus
● Antioch 638

Baghdad 762 ✖ Nehawand 641
● Ctesiphon 638

648

● Damascus 635
Qadisiya 637 ✖
✖ Basra 638

armuk 636 ✖
✖ Jerusalem 638
✖ Adzhnadein 634
✖ Heliopolis 640
● Cairo 641

Indus

✖ Ohod 625
● Medina 622
✖ Badr 624

● Mecca 630

TO EAST INDIES

TO ZANZIBAR

The expansion of Islam

▢	Conquests of Mohammed (to 632)
▢	Conquests of the First Four Caliphs (to 656)
▢	Conquests of the Omayyads (to 750)
▢	Subsequent Islamic expansion
✖	Muslim defeat
✕	Muslim victory
644	Date of occupation
(669)	Date of siege
➜	Main line of Arab expansion

37 The Arab World in Eclipse

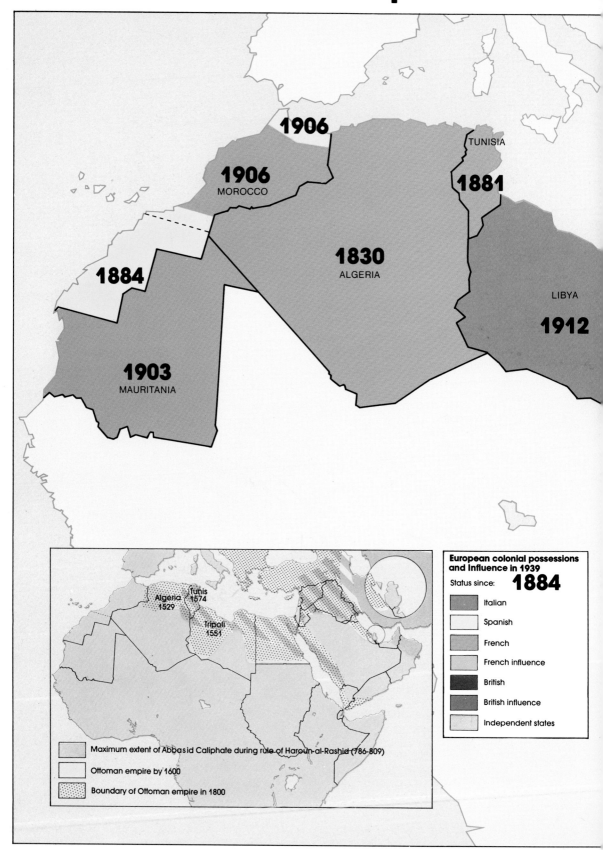

1906

1906
MOROCCO

1906

TUNISIA

1881

1884

1830
ALGERIA

LIBYA

1912

1903
MAURITANIA

**European colonial possessions
and influence in 1939**

Status since: **1884**

	Italian
	Spanish
	French
	French influence
	British
	British influence
	Independent states

Tunis
1574

Algeria
1529

Tripoli
1551

	Maximum extent of Abbasid Caliphate during rule of Haroun-al-Rashid (786-809)
	Ottoman empire by 1600
	Boundary of Ottoman empire in 1800

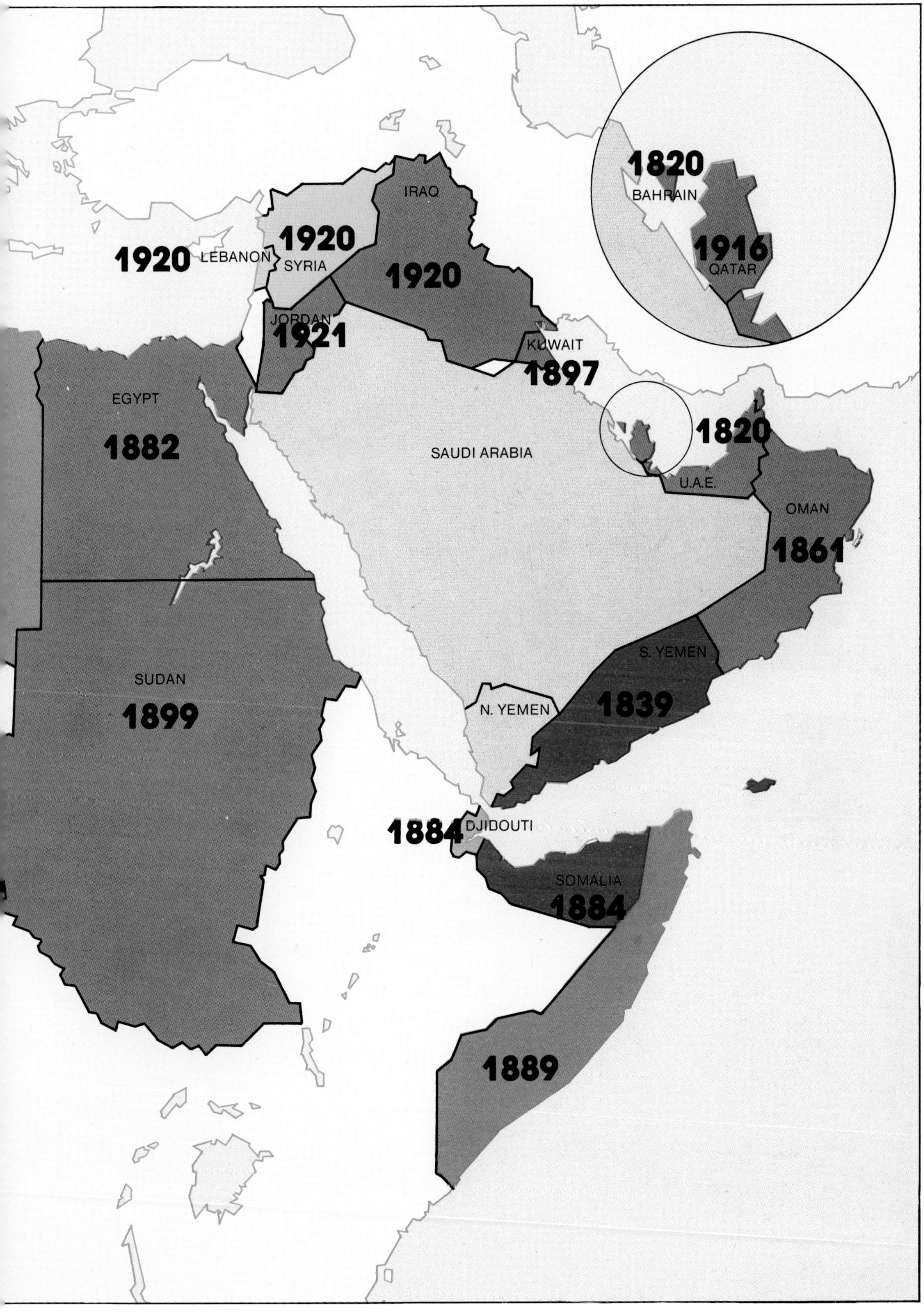

1820
BAHRAIN
1916
QATAR
IRAQ
1920
SYRIA
1920
LEBANON
1920
JORDAN
1921
KUWAIT
1897
EGYPT
1882
SAUDI ARABIA
1820
U.A.E.
OMAN
1861
S. YEMEN
1839
N. YEMEN
SUDAN
1899
1884
DJIBOUTI
SOMALIA
1884
1889

38 National Resurgence

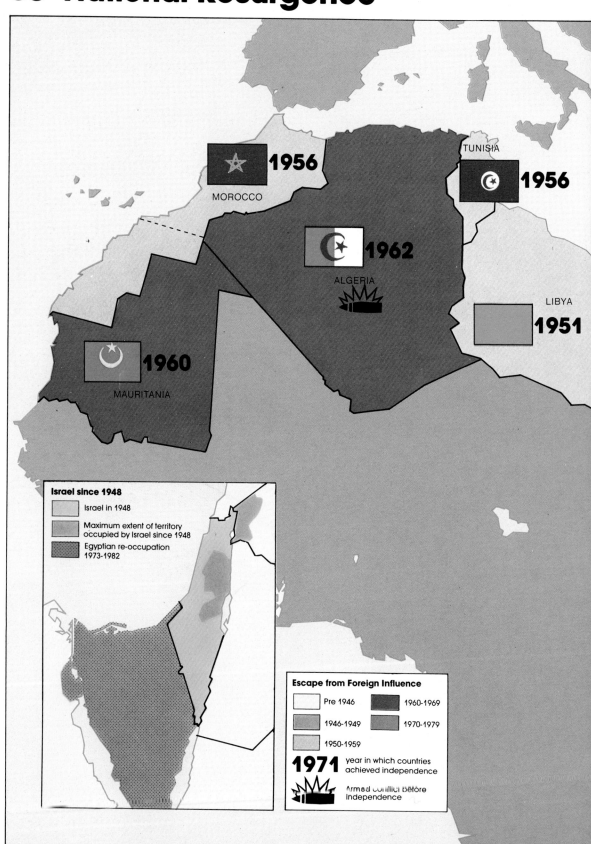

MOROCCO **1956**

TUNISIA **1956**

ALGERIA **1962**

LIBYA **1951**

MAURITANIA **1960**

Israel since 1948

Israel in 1948

Maximum extent of territory occupied by Israel since 1948

Egyptian re-occupation 1973-1982

Escape from Foreign Influence

Pre 1946

1946-1949

1950-1959

1960-1969

1970-1979

1971 year in which countries achieved independence

Armed conflict before independence

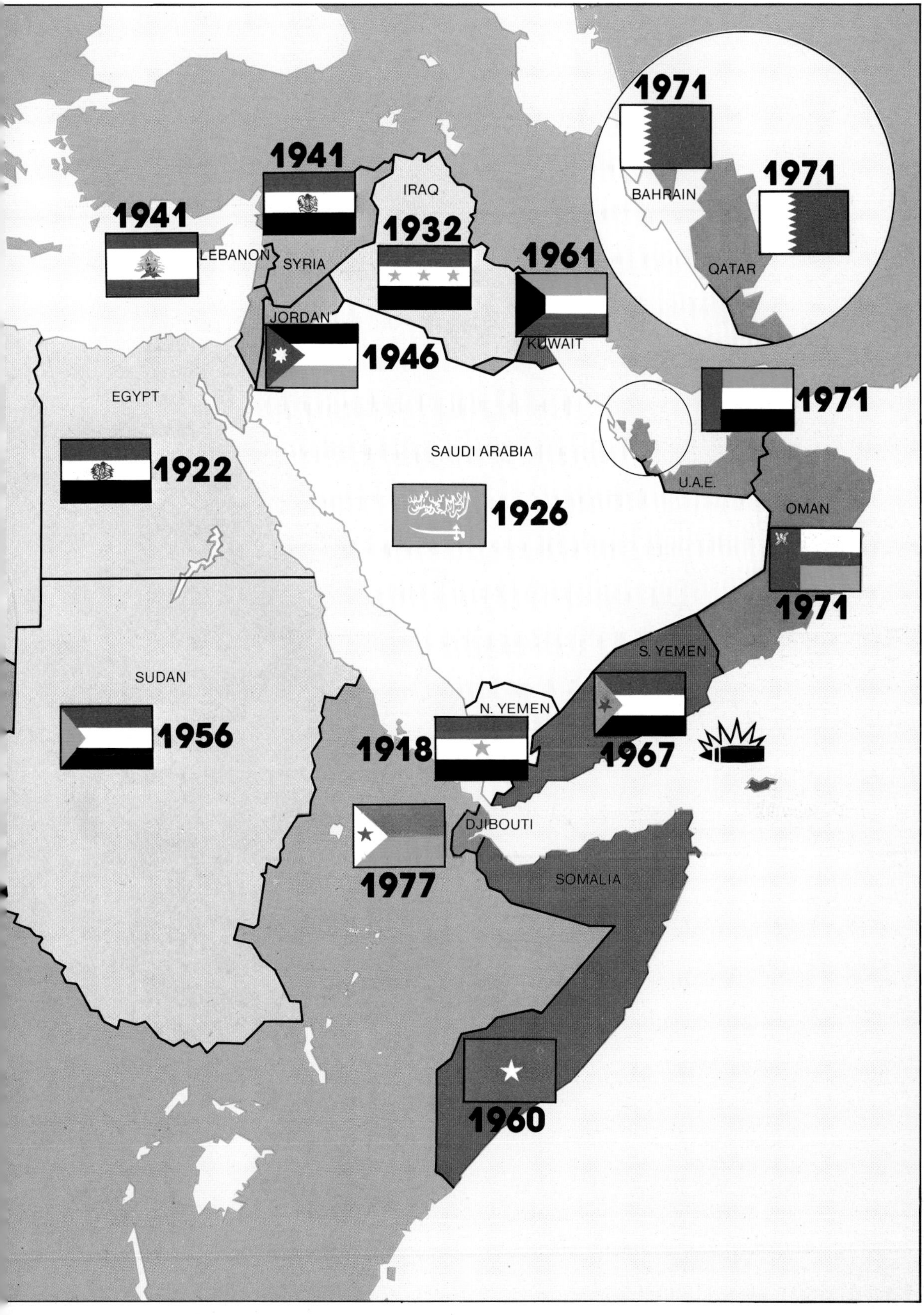

1941
LEBANON
1941
SYRIA
IRAQ
1932
JORDAN
1946
1961
KUWAIT
1971
BAHRAIN
1971
QATAR
1971
EGYPT
1922
SAUDI ARABIA
1926
U.A.E.
OMAN
1971
SUDAN
1956
S. YEMEN
N. YEMEN
1918
1967
DJIBOUTI
1977
SOMALIA
1960

Algeria

ALGERIA is the largest nation in north-western Africa.

THE LAND The Atlas region in the north covers about one-seventh of Algeria. It contains the Tell Atlas, or Maritime Zone, in the north-west. This region consists of mountain ranges, plateaux and fertile lowlands, including the Cheliff River valley and the Mitidja plain near Algiers. South of the Tell Atlas are high plateaux which contain large salt marshes, notably the Chott ech Chergui and the Chott el Hadna. Beyond these plateaux, the land rises to more than 2000 metres in the rugged Saharan Atlas range. The Tell Atlas, the plateaux and the Saharan Atlas merge in the north-east in a structurally complex region, comprising several highlands, such as the Grand Kabylie in the Djurdjura massif, and the Hodna, Aurès and Tebessa mountains in the south. The chief farming region is the Annaba plain.

The Sahara covers the rest of Algeria. In the north there are oases fed by water from the Saharan Atlas range and vast sand deserts. In the south-east is the volcanic Ahaggar massif which contains Mount Tahat (2918m above sea level), Algeria's highest peak.

The coastal region has a Mediterranean climate with an average annual temperature range of 9° to 24°C and an average annual rainfall varying between 760mm at Algiers to 380mm at Oran. Most rain falls in winter. Inland, the mountains are generally humid, although the high plateaux are semi-arid. Snow covers the Saharan Atlas peaks in winter, but the central Sahara has an average annual temperature range of 13°C to 37°C. The vegetation ranges from maquis in the far north, pine and oak forests in the wetter uplands, grassland on the high plateaux and sparse desert vegetation in the Sahara. The wildlife includes antelopes, gazelles and wild boars.

ECONOMY In 1980 Algeria had the highest total GNP (US $36,410 millions) in North Africa, while its per capita GNP was second only to that of Libya. Although 42 per cent of the people are engaged in agriculture, industry, particularly oil and natural gas extraction, dominates the economy. Algeria is Africa's top natural gas producer, with some of the world's largest reserves, and it ranks third in oil production. Algeria is rich in other minerals, including iron ore, lead, phosphates and zinc.

Farmland covers only 3 per cent of Algeria. Cereals, fruits, olives, tobacco, vegetables and vines occupy most of the farmland. Forests cover 2 per cent of the land and pasture about 15 per cent. In 1980 there were 12.5 million sheep, 2.85 million goats and 1.4 million cattle. In 1978 agriculture, forestry and fishing accounted for 8 per cent of the GDP, as opposed to 56 per cent from industry. Manufacturing, backed by government investment, has expanded greatly since independence, especially in the northern ports. The government controls heavy industry, but there is a sizeable private sector participation in light industry.

Railways link the main cities in the Tell Atlas. There are 3951km of railways and 82,000km of roads. Algeria has seven major oil pipeline systems and the leading ports include Algiers, Annaba, Arzew, Béjaia, Skikda and Oran. In recent years, Algeria's mineral exports have created generally favourable trade balances. France, West Germany and the United States are major trading partners.

PEOPLE In 1961-62 most of the million European settlers left Algeria. Although French is still spoken by educated Algerians, the government has pursued a policy of Arabization, particularly since 1968. Most people now speak Arabic, although about 20 per cent is of Berber origin, being descendants of the original people of the Maghreb. They include the Chaouia of the Aurès mountains, the Kabyles of the Grand Kabylie region, and the Tuaregs of the Sahara.

In 1970-78 the population increased by the extremely high rate of 3.2 per cent. This population explosion was caused partly by a marked reduction in the death rate and, as a result, the average life expectancy at birth rose from 47 years in 1960 to 56 in 1978. Partly reflecting the emphasis on industrialization, the urban population increased from 30 per cent of the total in 1960 to 61 per cent in 1980. This has created housing shortages and urban unemployment, factors that have encouraged emigration, mainly to France.

Social services, including national disease prevention campaigns, have been enlarged. About 83 per cent of children of primary school age and 29 per cent of secondary school age now attend school and the literacy rate is increasing. In the late 1970s, more than 3 million radio receivers and half a million television sets were in circulation. Of the four main daily newspapers, three are in Arabic and one in French.

HISTORY From the 1100s BC, Algeria came successively under Phoenician, Carthaginian and Roman rule. The Vandals took Algeria in AD 429, but the Byzantine Empire reconquered parts of it in the 500s. Islam was introduced in the 600s and was soon embraced by the overwhelming majority of the people. Arabic became the chief language, although Berber culture remained strong in rural inland areas.

Northern Algeria was part of the Ottoman Empire between 1518 and 1830, when France seized Algiers. French colonization was bitterly resisted, although Algeria was proclaimed a French territory in 1848.

After World War II, several nationalist organizations united to form the *Front de Libération Nationale* (FLN), which began open warfare against the French dominated government in 1954. A cease-fire was negotiated in 1962 and Algeria became independent on July 3, 1962. The first President, Mohammed Ben Bella, was deposed in 1965 by a Revolutionary

Founded in the tenth century, on the site of a Roman settlement, Algiers became the dominant Barbary state and then the capital of Algiers.

Council led by Colonel Houari Boumedienne. The 1976 Constitution restored elections which were held in 1977 and 1982. President Boumedienne died in 1978 and was succeeded by Benjedid Chadli.

GOVERNMENT Algeria is a one-party republic. The FLN, the only party, nominates the President and candidates for the National Assembly. The President and the 261 deputies in the National Assembly are then elected by universal suffrage. The President presides over the Council of Ministers.

Area: 2,381,741km²; **Population:** 20,042,000 (1982); **Capital:** Algiers (population 1977, 1,800,000); **Other cities:** Oran (500,000), Constantine (430,000), Annaba (340,000); **Official language:** Arabic; **Adult literacy rate:** 35% (1977); **Health:** 2 doctors per 10,000 people; 3 hospital beds per 1000 people; **Average life expectancy at birth:** 56 years; **Unit of currency:** Dinar; **Exports** (in order of value): fuels and lubricants (97.5% of the total in 1979), food and tobacco, primary products and raw materials; **Imports** (in order of value): capital goods, semi-finished goods, food and tobacco, consumer goods; **Per capita GNP:** US $1920 (1980).

Bahrain

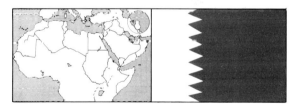

BAHRAIN is a small island nation in the Arabian (Persian) Gulf, about 30km from the coast of Saudi Arabia.

THE LAND Bahrain contains 33 islands, the largest of which is also called Bahrain. It is about 50km long and 13-25km wide and has a plentiful freshwater supply from springs and artesian wells. A causeway links Bahrain Island to the second largest island, Muharraq, which is about 6km long and 1.6km wide. Other islands include the Hawar group (near Qatar), Jidda, Sitra and Umm An-Nassan. The islands are sandy and low-lying. The highest point is Jabal ad-Dukhan, a hill on Bahrain Island that reaches 135 metres above sea level.

The average annual rainfall is only 80mm and most

of this falls in the mild winter months of December to March, when temperatures range between 16°C and 21°C. In summer, temperatures soar to around 43°C and the humidity is high. The land is mostly desert except around oases.

ECONOMY Bahrain has a booming economy and its 1979 per capita GNP was higher than those of Greece and Spain. Oil, first discovered in commercial quanitites in 1932, forms the basis of the economy. But production has been declining recently and the known reserves will run out in about 1995. As a result, the government has been diversifying the economy, encouraging the development of banking, trade, commerce, shipping and manufacturing, with the aim of making Bahrain the 'Singapore' of the Middle East. For example, the smelter of Aluminium Bahrain (ALBA), opened in 1971, became the largest Middle Eastern industrial complex not concerned with oil. The government now holds a majority shareholding in ALBA. In fact, Bahraini nationals must hold a majority of the shares in all companies except banks. Another recent development has been the establishment of the Arab Shipbuilding and Repair Yard (ASRY), which is jointly owned by Bahrain, Iraq, Kuwait, Libya, Qatar, Saudi Arabia and the UAE. Natural gas production is increasing — the gas was once wastefully flared — and consumer goods industries have been expanding.

Traditional industries, such as dhow building and pearl fishing, are still carried on, but they have declined in recent times. Farmland and pasture make up about 11 per cent of the country, and agriculture and fishing employ 6.5 per cent of the work force. Dates, fruits, vegetables and fodder crops are produced. There are 13,000 goats, 5000 cattle, 3000 sheep and 1000 camels.

Transport facilities have been extended in recent years and a causeway linking Bahrain to Saudi Arabia is due to be completed by 1985. The chief port is Mina Sulman, south of Manama. Bahrain's international airport, on the Europe-southern Asia-Australia route, is on Muharraq Island.

PEOPLE Bahrain is the most densely populated Gulf state and, in 1970-79, its population was increasing by the high rate of 7.2 per cent per year. Part of this increase was caused by immigration, because economic expansion and the absence of taxation has attracted many people from such countries as India, Iran, Pakistan, South Korea, the UK and the USA. (In 1980 an estimated 37 per cent of the population was foreign.) Most Bahraini nationals are of Arab origin, although perhaps one-fifth are of Iranian descent.

Much of the revenue from oil sales has been used to develop public works and social services, including free education and health services. Bahrain has four daily newspapers, two in Arabic and two in English. The government-owned Bahrain Broadcasting Station transmits programmes in Arabic, while the commercial Radio Bahrain broadcasts in English. In 1980 there were 100,000 radio and 80,000 television receiving sets in circulation.

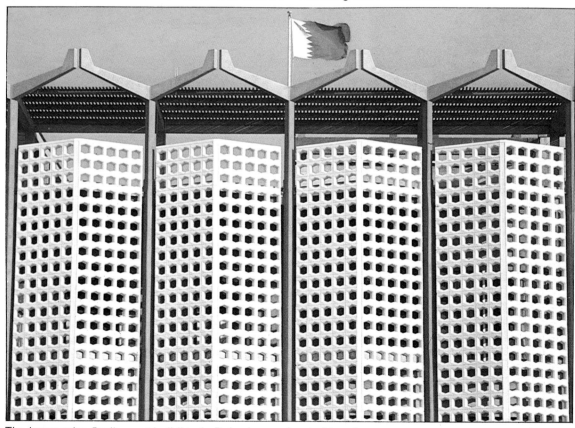

The impressive Parliament building in Bahrain was funded by oil revenues.

HISTORY Archaeologists have discovered that Bahrain was a flourishing trading centre as early as 2000 BC. It was occupied by Arabs in the 7th century AD and it served as a Portuguese base from 1521 to 1602. From 1602 it came intermittently under the control of Persia, but the Persians were expelled in 1783. British influence increased in the 19th century and, to counter claims by Iran and Turkey, Bahrain came under British protection in 1861. Full independence was achieved in 1971 when Bahrain became a member of the Arab League and the United Nations.

GOVERNMENT The Emir, Sheikh Isa bin Sulman al-Khalifa, who succeeded to the throne in 1961, is a member of the dynasty that has ruled Bahrain since 1783. Today the Cabinet, headed by a prime minister appointed by the Emir, administers the country. The 1973 Constitution provided for a National Assembly consisting of the Cabinet and 30 members elected to four-year terms by popular vote. There are no political parties and all candidates must be independents. A National Assembly was elected in December 1973, but it was dissolved in August 1975.

Area: 622km²; **Population:** 485,000 (1982); **Capital:** Manama (population 1978, 114,000); **Other urban areas:** Muharraq Town (48,000); **Official language:** Arabic; **Adult literacy rate:** 39% (1977); **Health:** 8 doctors per 10,000 people; 4 hospital beds per 1000 people; **Unit of currency:** Dinar. **Exports** (in order of value): petroleum and products, machinery and transport equipment, non-ferrous metals, clothing; **Imports** (in order of value): petroleum and products, machinery and transport equipment, manufactured goods, food and live animals; **Per capita GNP:** US $5560 (1980).

Djibouti

DJIBOUTI is a republic on the strait of Bab al Mandab which links the Red Sea to the Gulf of Aden. It was formerly called French Somaliland and also the French Territory of the Afars and Issas.

THE LAND Djibouti occupies an area that is part of the East African Rift Valley system. It contains high, uplifted blocks, reaching 2063 metres in the north, depressions, such as the salt lake Assal, 174 metres below sea level, and volcanic wastelands behind the narrow coastal plain. The climate is hot and arid. The average annual rainfall is generally under 120mm, the rainy season being October-April. Desert covers most of Djibouti, and only 0.1 per cent is cultivated.

A traditional mosque in Djibouti, one of the newest and poorest of the Arab nations.

ECONOMY Djibouti is a poor country and most people are nomadic herdsmen. In 1980 there were 522,000 goats, 317,000 sheep and 33,000 cattle. Cattle and skins are the main exports. Sea-fishing is also important. The port of Djibouti is the terminus of a railway extending to Addis Ababa in Ethiopia and duties levied on Ethiopian trade and services provided to ocean-going ships are important sources of income. Djibouti also has an international airport. The closure of the Suez Canal (1967-75) and the Ethiopian-Somali conflict in the late 1970s reduced Djibouti's income, but aid has come from Saudi Arabia, France and other sources.

PEOPLE In 1980 an estimated 47 per cent of the people were Issas (a Somali clan, mainly in the south), 37 per cent were Afars (or Danakils, mainly in the north), 8 per cent were Europeans (mostly French), and 6 per cent were Arabs. The country is thinly populated but in 1970-79 the population increased by 8.2 per cent per year. Djibouti has a radio and a television station. In 1977 there were 30,000 radio and 10,000 television sets in circulation.

HISTORY France began to take an interest in the area in 1859. The port of Djibouti was built in 1884 and, in 1897-1917, French engineers built the railway to Addis Ababa. Djibouti became a French overseas territory in 1946, but it gained full independence on June 27, 1977. Hassan Gouled Aptidon, an Issa, became the first President. Djibouti remained neutral in the Ethiopian-Somali conflict.

GOVERNMENT Executive power is vested in the President and the Council of Ministers. The Chamber of Deputies, elected in 1977 on a single list presented by the *Rassemblement Populaire pour l'Indépendance*, comprises 33 Issas, 30 Afars and 2 Arabs.

Area: 22,000km²; **Population:** 371,000 (1982); **Capital:** Djibouti (population 1981, 150,000); **Official language:** French; **Health:** 6 doctors per 10,000 people; 9 hospital beds per 1000 people; **Unit of currency:** Djibouti franc; **Exports** (in order of value): cattle, skins and leather, **Imports** (in order of value): textiles, machinery and transport equipment, dairy products; **Per capita GNP:** US $480 (1980).

Egypt

EGYPT, in north-eastern Africa, is officially called the Araba Republic of Egypt (ARE).

THE LAND There are four main land regions. The Sinai peninsula in the north-east is bounded by the Suez Canal and the Gulf of Suez in the west, and the Gulf of Aqaba in the east. In the north, a low plain borders the Mediterranean Sea. The Land rises to the south, where Egypt's highest peak, Gebel Katherina, reaches 2637 metres.

The eastern desert, east of the Nile valley, consists of rocky plateaux and a rugged mountain range overlooking the Red Sea.

The western desert covers more than three-fifths of Egypt. It is mostly below 200 metres and includes several deep basins. The Qattara Depression reaches 133 metres below sea level. The main uplands are in the south-west. The western desert has several major oases (Dakhla, Faiyum, Farafra, Kharga and Siwa) and there is much potential for economic development.

The fourth region, the Nile valley, contains the man-made Lake Nasser which is held back by the Aswan High Dam in the south. Below Aswan, the valley is narrow, but it gradually broadens out in Middle Egypt. North of Cairo, the Nile divides into two main branches, the Damietta and Rosetta which flow through the triangular-shaped delta which was formed from river-borne sediment. The delta covers about 22,000sq km, but little silt is now carried by the Nile; most of it is trapped behind the Aswan High Dam. The Nile is Egypt's main source of water.

The climate is arid. The northern coast, the wettest area, has only about 200mm of rain per year. Parts of the south have virtually no rain. Summers are extremely hot and winters warm. Large diurnal ranges are common. Most of Egypt is desert and there are no forests and little pasture. The character-istic plant around oases is the date palm. Wildlife is sparse.

ECONOMY Egypt is Africa's second most industrialized nation, but it has a comparatively low per capita GNP. Its chief mineral resources include petroleum and natural gas, phosphates, iron ore, manganese and salt. Agriculture is the chief activity, although farmland covers only 3 per cent of the land. The chief crop is cotton, and cotton and cotton goods are the leading exports. Cereals, fruits, rice, sugar-cane, vegetables and fodder crops are also grown. In 1980 Egypt had 2 million cattle, 1.7 million sheep and 1.7 million goats. Most industry is nationalized, although foreign investment in joint-venture projects has been welcomed since 1974. Manufactures include cotton goods, refined sugar, cement, chemicals and plastics, and steel, which has been developed with cheap electricity from the Aswan High Dam. There are also various assembly industries.

The 173km-long Suez Canal is a major source of income, although it was blocked in 1967-75. Internal transport facilities include more than 90,000km of roads and nearly 5000km of railways. Alexandria is the chief port. More than a million tourists visited Egypt in 1979 and tourism is an important source of foreign exchange. Leading trade partners include Italy, the USA, West Germany, France and the UK. Egypt's economy has suffered in recent years from adverse trade balances and large annual debt repayments. But the economy became more buoyant in the early 1980s.

PEOPLE While the annual rate of population increase has dropped in recent years, it was still estimated at 2.0 per cent in 1970-79, a rate that would double the population in 35 years. About 99 per cent of the people live in about 35,000sq. km in the fertile, irrigated Nile valley, one of the world's most densely populated regions. In 1980, 45 per cent of the people lived in urban areas, as compared with 30 per cent in 1947.

Arabic is the official language and most people are Egyptian Arabs, although there are small Berber minorities in the western desert and Nubian and Sudanese communities in the south. About 90 per cent of the people are Muslims. The Copts form the largest religious minority. Social services are increasing and the average life expectancy at birth rose by 8 years between 1960 and 1980. Primary education has been compulsory since 1933. There are 12 universities; the Al-Azhar Koranic University, established in AD 972, is the world's oldest. Although more than half of the adult population is illiterate, six daily newspapers are published in Alexandria and ten in Cairo. In 1978 there were 5.3 million radio and 1.1 million television sets in circulation in Egypt.

HISTORY Ancient Egypt was one of the world's greatest early civilizations. The first of the 30 dynasties that ruled it was founded in about 3100 BC when Upper and Lower Egypt were united. Ancient Egypt reached the peak of its glory under King Thutmose III in 1490-1436 BC. From 525 BC Egypt was mostly under foreign rule, including that of the Persians, Greeks

Irrigation is the lifeblood of Egyptian agriculture. Picturesque but well-proven methods have been supplemented by vast schemes such as the Aswan High Dam.

and Romans. Islam was introduced during the Arab conquest of Egypt in AD 639-642.

Egypt was part of the Ottoman Empire from 1517 to 1798, but the country's modern history began in 1805 when Mehemet Ali, a former Albanian officer, became governor and began to modernize Egypt. In 1881 Britain occupied the country and declared it a protectorate in 1914. Egypt became an independent monarchy in 1922, although British troops remained. In 1948-49 Egypt fought alongside other Arab nations against the creation of the state of Israel. The monarchy was overthrown in 1952 and General Muhammad Neguib became President. In 1954, however, Colonel Abdel Nasser took over and Britain agreed to withdraw its forces. In 1956 President Nasser nationalized the Suez Canal. Anglo-French and Israeli troops attacked Egypt but soon withdrew. Egypt was involved in wars with Israel in 1967 and again in 1973, by which time Colonel Muhammad Anwar as-Sadat had become President, Nasser having died in 1970. Sadat negotiated a peace treaty with Israel in 1979, but he was assassinated in 1981. His successor was General Muhammad Hosni Mubarak. Under the peace treaty, the Sinai peninsula was returned to Egypt by 1982.

GOVERNMENT Egypt is a democratic, socialist Arab Republic. The President exercises executive authority and is assisted by a Council of Ministers. The People's Assembly has 392 members, most of whom are elected by universal suffrage to five-year terms.

Area: 1,001,449km²; **Population:** 41,380,000 (1982); **Capital:** Cairo (population with suburbs 1979, 8,539,000); **Other cities** (1976 populations): Alexandria (2,318,000), El Giza (1,230,000), Subra-El Khema (349,000), El Mahalla el Kubra (292,000), Tanta (283,000), Port Said (263,000), El Mansura (259,000); **Official language:** Arabic; **Adult literacy rate:** 44% (1977); **Health:** 9 doctors per 10,000 people; 2 hospital beds per 1000 people; **Average life expectancy at birth:** 54 years; **Unit of currency:** Egyptian pound; **Exports** (in order of value): raw cotton, petroleum and petroleum products, cotton yarn and fabrics, rice, fruits; **Imports** (in order of value): machinery and electrical apparatus, food, mineral products, transport equipment; **Per capita GNP:** US $580 (1980).

Iraq

IRAQ is a large Arab republic in south-western Asia.

THE LAND There are three main land regions. The Tigris-Euphrates lowlands, formerly called Mesopotamia, is the largest alluvial tract in the Middle East. Both rivers rise in Turkey and, in their upper courses in Iraq, they are fast flowing. Between them is a plain, the Jezirah, which rises to 1547 metres near the Syrian border. Below Ramadi and Baghdad, however, the gradient changes and the rivers wind sluggishly across nearly flat plains, often changing their courses when in flood. About 190km from the Arabian Gulf, the rivers join to form the navigable Shatt al-Arab.

The second land region is the highland zone east of the Tigris, which rises to more than 3000 metres near the Iranian border. The western desert, or Hamad, reaches a maximum height of about 1000 metres.

Iran has hot summers, but December to March can be cold. For example, Basra has an average annual temperature range of 11°C (January) to 35°C (July). At Baghdad the range is 9°-34°C, while at Mosul it is 5°-35°C. The north-eastern uplands are the wettest region, with an average annual rainfall of 400 to 600mm. The rest of the country is arid and all farmland must be irrigated. For instance, Baghdad has about 140mm of rain per year and Basra 170mm. Desert covers western Iraq. The lower Tigris-Euphrates lowland contains much swamp vegetation, including reed marshes and palm belts. Grassland covers the Jezirah and parts of the north-eastern uplands, where most of Iraq's woodlands are also found.

ECONOMY Iraq has the second highest total GNP in the Arab world (US $39,500 million in 1980), but it ranks 8th according to its per capita GNP. The economy is based on oil and Iraq is the Arab world's second largest producer, after Saudi Arabia. Iraq also produces natural gas and other minerals. The oil industry is government-owned and the massive reserves were estimated to be 31,100 million million barrels in 1980. Farmland covers 12 per cent of the land, pasture another 9 per cent and woodland 3½ per cent, but agriculture is a major industry. The chief food crops are wheat, barley, rice, fruits and vegetables, while dates and cotton are the chief cash crops. Sheep and goats are reared mainly in the north, while cattle are kept in the south to supply milk and serve as draught animals.

Manufacturing is developing rapidly, especially in Baghdad and Mosul. The chief port is Basra. In 1975 there were 11,859km of roads and 1955km of railways.

Oil exports gave Iraq favourable trade balances, at least until the outbreak of war with Iran in 1980, and Iraq is the Arab world's third largest aid donor to developing countries, after Saudi Arabia and Kuwait. Most trade is with Europe, Japan and the USA. In 1977 nearly 600,000 tourists visited Iraq.

PEOPLE Iraq's population increased by 3.4 per cent per year in 1970-79, a rate that would double the population in only 21 years. There has also been a marked migration from rural areas to cities and towns, especially Baghdad. In 1980 72 per cent of the people lived in urban areas, as opposed to 43 per cent in 1960. About 95 per cent of the people are Muslims. Ethnically, an estimated 79 per cent are Arabs, 16 per cent are Kurds (in the north-east), 3 per cent are Persian and 2 per cent are Turkish.

The government has recently extended its social services, particularly education which is now free at primary and secondary levels. There are six universities. Five daily newspapers are published in Baghdad. In 1980 there were 2.1 million radios and 625,000 television sets in circulation.

The Kamidyah mosque, Baghdad. More than 95% of Iraqis are Muslims.

HISTORY The Tigris-Euphrates lowlands were the centre for several early civilizations, including those of the Sumerians, Babylonians, Assyrians and Chaldeans. Islam was introduced in AD 634-641.

Iraq was a backward part of the Ottoman Empire from 1638 until World War I. In 1920 Iraq was created as a monarchy, with Faisal I becoming king. The country was ruled at first under a British mandate, but full independence was achieved in 1932. In 1948 troops from Iraq were involved in the Arab-Israeli war and they also participated in later wars.

In 1958 the monarchy was overthrown and Iraq came under military rule. The 1960s were marred by fighting in the north-east with Kurdish nationalists who wanted to establish a separate state with Kurds in Iran, Turkey and the USSR. The 1970s saw further conflict, although regional autonomy was granted to Kurdistan in 1974 and a 50-member Kurdish Legislative Council was elected in 1980.

The 1970s also witnessed generally bad relations with Iran, partly because of Iran's claims on part of the Shatt al-Arab channel, and its annexation of two islands (Abu Musa and Tumb) in 1971. War broke out in 1980 when Iraqi troops entered Iran. The war continued intermittently into 1982.

GOVERNMENT Supreme power is vested in the Council of the Revolutionary Command Council, which elects the President. The only legal party is the National Progressive Front which was a coalition between the Arab Baath Socialist Party and the Iraq Communist Party, until the Communists withdrew in 1979. A 250-member National Assembly, elected in 1980, is dominated by the ruling Baathist group.

Area: 434,924km²; **Population:** 13,976,000 (1982); **Capital:** Baghdad (population 1977, 3,206,000); **Other cities** (1970 populations): Basra (334,000), Mosul (293,000); **Official language:** Arabic; **Adult literacy rate:** 27% (1977); **Health:** 5 doctors per 10,000 people; 2 hospital beds per 1000 people; **Average life expectancy at birth:** 55 years; **Unit of currency:** Iraqi dinar; **Exports** (in order of value): crude petroleum (98% of the total in 1973-77), dates, hides and skins; **Imports** (in order of value): boilers and engines, automobiles and parts, sugar, pharmaceutical products; **Per capita GNP:** US $3020 (1980).

Jordan

JORDAN is a constitutional monarchy, officially called the Hashemite Kingdom of Jordan.

THE LAND After the Arab-Israeli War of 1948, Jordan contained a fertile upland, called the West Bank region, west of the River Jordan and the Dead Sea. This region, formerly part of Arab Palestine, has been occupied by Israel since 1967.

The Jordan valley is part of the huge Rift Valley system that extends southwards to the Red Sea and eastern Africa. The northern end of the valley is just above sea level, but the shoreline of the Dead Sea is 393 metres below sea level, the world's lowest exposed land depression. The deepest part of the Dead Sea is 792 metres below the level of the Mediterranean Sea. The Rift valley floor above the Dead Sea is called Al Ghor.

East of the Rift Valley is the uptilted rim of the northern part of the Arabian plateau, a zone called the Jordanian Highlands. East of these dissected highlands is undulating country merging into flat plains. Jordan's highest point is Jabal Ram, which reaches 1754 metres above sea level north-east of Aqaba which is Jordan's only outlet to the sea.

Jordan has a hot climate. The West Bank and the highlands north and west of Amman have a Mediterranean climate and an average annual rainfall between 380 and 1000mm. But more than four-fifths of Jordan is barren desert.

ECONOMY The Arab-Israeli wars disrupted Jordan's economy, but steady growth was achieved throughout the 1970s and early 1980s. Jordan has benefited from improved relations with the rest of the Arab world, from substantial foreign aid, particularly from Saudi Arabia, Iraq, Kuwait, Qatar and the UAE, from handling increased transit trade, especially since the start of the Iraq-Iran war in 1980, from remittances from Jordanians working in Gulf countries, and from skilful economic management in a comparatively stable political situation. The country's leading resource is phosphates, but Jordan also has other minerals, some unexploited as yet. Agriculture contributes 11 per cent of the GDP, although only 14 per cent of the country can be farmed. The chief agricultural areas are the highlands north of Amman and the irrigated East Ghor. The chief crops are barley, fruits, including grapes and olives, vegetables and wheat. In 1980 there were 380,000 goats, 280,000 sheep and 110,000 cattle. Manufacturing is increasing.

Aqaba is the only port. In 1980 there were 595km of railways and 4690km of roads, but lack of transport facilities is an obstacle to development. Import suppliers include Saudi Arabia, West Germany, the UK and the USA, while leading export markets are Saudi Arabia, Iraq and Syria. Tourism declined after 1967, but recovered in the 1970s when Jordan permitted visitors to cross to the West Bank. In 1980 there were 1,635,000 tourists in Jordan.

PEOPLE Population figures have been distorted in recent years by the presence of large numbers of Palestinian refugees. About 90 per cent of the people are Arabs and the vast majority is Muslim. There is a Christian minority. In 1980 56 per cent of the people lived in urban areas. There are still some nomadic herdsmen.

Social services are steadily increasing, and 90 per cent of primary school-age children and 70 per cent of secondary school-age children now attend school. Five daily newspapers are published in Amman. In 1980 there were 200,000 radio and 180,000 television sets in circulation on the East Bank.

HISTORY The Romans occupied what is now northern Jordan in 64 BC and they also took the southern kingdom of the Arabian Nabataeans in AD 106. The area became part of the Islamic Empire in 636. From the start of the 16th century, Jordan was part of the Ottoman Empire, but after World War I, Transjordan, as Jordan was then called, and Palestine were jointly ruled by Britain under a League of Nations mandate. In 1921 Amir Abdullah was recognized as the ruler of Transjordan and, in 1923, Transjordan became a separate nation under British protection.

The Street of Facades in Petra, an ancient, ruined, rock city carved in rose and purple limestone.

The mandate was ended after World War II. In 1948 Jordanian and other Arab armies entered Palestine to help the Palestinian Arabs, believing that they should govern Palestine after Britain's withdrawal. When the war ended, the West Bank became part of Jordan. Many Palestinian refugees flooded into Jordan and Palestinian guerrilla bases were established. After a series of aircraft hijacks and an attempted assassination of King Hussein, who had succeeded in 1952, the Jordanian army sought to expel the Palestinian guerrillas and a civil war ensued in 1970-71. In 1973 King Hussein declared a general amnesty for Palestinians and, in 1974, an Arab Summit Conference in Rabat declared the Palestinian Liberation Organization (PLO) to be the sole legal representative of the Palestinian people. Accordingly, King Hussein ceded Jordan's claim to the West Bank to the PLO.

GOVERNMENT According to the Constitution, Jordan has a Parliament consisting of a 30-member Senate appointed by the King and an elected 60-member House of Representatives. However, in 1974, Parliament approved Constitutional amendments enabling the King to dissolve parliament and, in 1976, he was empowered to postpone elections indefinitely. In its place, a 60-member National Consultative Council was appointed by the King to serve 2-year terms.

Area: 97,740km²; **Population:** 3,475,000 (1982); **Capital:** Amman (population 1979, 649,000); **Other cities:** Zarka (216,000); **Official language:** Arabic; **Adult literacy rate:** 59% (1977); **Health:** 5 doctors per 10,000 people; 1 hospital bed per 1000 people; **Average life expectancy at birth:** 56 years; **Unit of currency:** Jordanian dinar; **Exports** (in order of value): phosphates, vegetables and fruit, cigarettes; **Imports** (in order of value): consumer goods, raw materials including fuel and oil, machinery and transport equipment; **Per capita GNP:** US $1420 (1980), for the East Bank only.

Kuwait

KUWAIT, a monarchy on the north-western corner of the Arabian (Persian) Gulf, was formerly a poor country with an economy based on trading, fishing and animal husbandry. But since 1946, when large-scale oil production began, it has become one of the world's richest nations.

THE LAND Most of Kuwait is flat or gently undulating. The highest land is in the south and west, where a maximum height of about 275 metres is reached. The north-east includes part of the Shatt al-Arab delta, while nearby is the large Kuwait Bay.

The land is arid; there are no permanent streams. The average annual rainfall varies between about 10mm in the south to 370mm in the north, but it is unreliable. Rain falls mainly in winter. The average annual temperature range is between 10°C and 32°C, although summer temperatures may soar to 49°C and frosts may occur in winter. The vegetation is sparse except around oases. Marsh vegetation grows along parts of the coast and there is some grassland inland.

The striking and renowned Kuwaiti water towers. Most of the drinking water is distilled from sea water.

ECONOMY In 1980 Kuwait had the world's third largest per capita GNP, after Qatar and the UAE. The chief resources are oil, which accounted for 72 per cent of Kuwait's GDP in 1979, and natural gas. Kuwait is south-western Asia's third largest oil producer and it has some of the world's biggest proven reserves. Less than 0.1 per cent of the land is farmed and only 7.5 per cent is pasture. Vegetables and dates are grown, but Kuwait imports most of its food. In 1980 there were 149,000 sheep, 103,000 goats and 10,000 cattle. More than half of the people work in service industries, 21 per cent work in construction industries, 13 per cent are in mining and manufacturing and 3½ per cent in farming. The construction industry has expanded with massive government investment in housing, new towns, roads, ports, desalination plants (which supply 90 per cent of Kuwait's fresh water), power stations and hotels. Manufacturing is dominated by oil-related industries. Cement, chemicals, paints, plastics and various consumer goods are also produced. The government is using oil revenue to diversify the economy and it also invests massively overseas. The chief ports include Kuwait City, Shuwaikh, Shualbah and Mina al-Ahmadi, an oil port. Kuwait City has a spectacular new international airport. In 1980 Kuwait had 1920km of roads.

The chief sources of imports are Japan, the USA and the UK. The leading export markets are Japan, Italy, the Netherlands and the UK.

PEOPLE In 1937 Kuwait had a population of 75,000 and Kuwait City was the chief town. By 1980 the population had reached 1,353,000, 88 per cent of whom lived in urban areas. The great expansion of population (at a rate of 6.2 per cent per year in 1970-79) results partly from a high rate of natural increase and partly from immigration. In 1980 an estimated 58.5 per cent of the people were non-Kuwaitis, mostly from other Arab nations.

Most Kuwait nationals are Muslim Arabs. They enjoy one of the world's most elaborate welfare systems. There is free education, including free food and clothing for students, free health services, a government job for anyone who cannot find another, land developed by the government and then sold to citizens at deflated prices, cheap petrol (Kuwait has more cars than any other country in relation to its population), and free local telephone calls. Kuwait is also a major aid donor to other Arab countries and to the developing world.

There are seven daily newspapers and, in the late 1970s, there were 700,000 radio and 200,000 television sets in circulation. Colour television was introduced in 1973.

HISTORY In historic times Kuwait was oriented more towards the nomadic culture of the Arabian peninsula rather than the farming cultures to the north. Arabs founded the port of Kuwait at the beginning of the 18th century and Kuwait flourished after the accession of the present ruling family of al-Sabah in 1756. In 1899 a treaty made Britain responsible for Kuwait's foreign affairs. This treaty remained in force until 1961 when Kuwait became fully independent.

Kuwait's first elections took place in 1961 and a National Assembly was elected in 1963. The National Assembly was dissolved in 1976, but a new 50-member National Assembly was elected in 1981, although the suffrage was limited and the radical element in the 1976 Assembly was eliminated.

GOVERNMENT Kuwait is a hereditary monarchy. Its 1962 Constitution was modified in 1976, with the suspension of the articles on the National Assembly, and again in 1980, with a decree concerning a new National Assembly elected by a franchise limited to 90,000 'first-class' citizens.

Area: 17,818km²; **Population:** 1,526,000 (1982); **Capital:** Kuwait City (population 1975, 78,000); **Other cities:** Hawalli (131,000), Salmiya (114,000); **Official language:** Arabic; **Adult literacy rate:** 60% (1977); **Health:** 13 doctors per 10,000 people; 4 hospital beds per 1000 people; **Average life expectancy at birth:** 69 years; **Unit of currency:** Kuwait dinar; **Exports** (in order of value): mineral fuels and lubricants (92% of the total in 1975-78), machinery and transport equipment, manufactured goods, chemicals; **Imports** (in order of value): machinery and transport equipment, manufactured goods, food and live animals; **Per capita GNP:** US $22,840 (1980).

Lebanon

LEBANON is an Arab republic bordering the Mediterranean Sea.

THE LAND Behind the coastal plain, which is up to 6km wide, are the Lebanon Mountains which reach 3083 metres at Qornet as Sauda, south-east of Tripoli. East of these mountains is a narrow plateau containing the fertile Bekaa valley and the headwaters of the Orontes River which flows north and the Litani River which flows south. In the far east the Anti-Lebanon Mountains rise to 2814 metres at Mount Hermon on the Syrian border.

Lebanon has the hot, dry summers and mild, moist winters that are characteristic of Mediterranean lands, except in the higher mountains. The average annual rainfall at Beirut is 920mm, although parts of the mountains have up to 2300mm and snow covers the highest peaks for half the year. Generally, however, the rainfall decreases from west to east. The Bekaa valley has 380mm a year and irrigation is practised.

The vegetation varies from subtropical to alpine. Acacia, cork oak and pines are the characteristic trees, but few of the famous cedars of Lebanon remain.

ECONOMY Lebanon has few resources, but in normal times it is prosperous with valuable entrepôt and tourist trades. And its businessmen are energetic entrepreneurs who have made Lebanon an international financial centre. However, since the 1975-76 civil war, the economy has been severely disrupted.

Farmland makes up about 34 per cent of the country and forests 7 per cent. In 1975, agriculture, forestry and fishing employed about 17 per cent of the workforce, manufacturing 18 per cent, and service industries most of the other people. The chief crops are citrus fruits, grapes, bananas, sugar beet, olives and wheat. The chief farming regions are the coastal plain and the Bekaa valley. In 1980 Lebanon had 380,000 goats, 280,000 sheep and 110,000 cattle. However, food must be imported. Manufacturing has suffered severely from recent violence, but oil refineries still provide Lebanon with cheap fuel.

The chief ports are Beirut and Tripoli, and Beirut has a major international airport. There are 355km of railways and 7100km of roads. In normal times, Lebanon has an adverse visible balance of trade, but such invisibles as services, tourism, transit trade and remittances from citizens abroad provide much revenue. Since 1975, however, the tourist industry has virtually collapsed. In 1977 most of Lebanon's imports came from Europe, while the Arab world took most of the exports.

PEOPLE UN sources suggest that Lebanon's population fell during the 1970s because of emigration. Internal conflict has arisen partly because of religious divisions. Probably more than half of the people today are Muslims or Druses (in 1958 there were 88,000 Druses, who dislike Muslims and Christians alike), while most of the rest are Christians, predominantly Maronites. Conflict between religious groups is deep-seated in Lebanese society and was the cause of the 1975-76 civil war. Arabs make up 90 per cent of the population and there are Armenian, Kurdish, Assyrian, Jewish, Greek and Turkish minorities. Lebanon also contains Palestinian refugees (187,500 in 1973). Their activities have led to border clashes and Israeli incursions into southern Lebanon.

Lebanon has had free primary education since 1960 and its adult literacy rate is the highest in the Arab world. Health standards are high and the average life expectancy at birth is second only to Kuwait in south-western Asia. There are about 40 daily newspapers, three of which are in Armenian, three in French and two in English. In the late 1970s about 605,000 radios and 425,000 television sets were in circulation.

HISTORY Lebanon was the base of the great Phoenician trading empire which reached its peak in the 12th to 9th centuries BC. From the early 16th century, the area was nominally part of the Ottoman empire. In 1858 Maronite peasants revolted against their Maronite overlords. The Druses, fearing that their Maronite serfs might also rebel, attacked the Maronites who appealed for help to Britain and

The fertile Bekaa valley is one of the chief farming regions of Lebanon, with many small vineyards and wheatfields.

France, who made Turkey establish a Maronite area with a Christian governor.

By the end of World War I, British and French forces had occupied Lebanon and, in 1920, the League of Nations mandated France to govern it. The Free French proclaimed Lebanon's independence in 1941, but full independence was not achieved until 1946 when all French troops were evacuated. In 1948 Lebanon was involved in the Arab-Israeli war.

Recent history has been marred by civil conflict and border clashes with Israel. In 1958 the USA helped to restore the government after an outbreak of fighting and, in 1969 and 1973, Lebanese forces clashed with militant Palestinians. In 1975-76 there was a bitter civil war between private Christian and Muslim armies. In 1976 a Syrian and, later, an Arab peace-keeping force helped to restore order. In 1978 Israel invaded southern Lebanon and a UN peace-keeping force of 6000 was established to act as a buffer between Lebanon and Israel. Fighting continued intermittently, and in June 1982 Israel launched an invasion in retaliation for various Palestinian actions.

GOVERNMENT Executive power is vested in the President, who must be a Maronite Christian, and who is elected for 6-year terms. The President appoints the Prime Minister, who must be a Sunni Muslim, and the Cabinet, which must reflect the balance in the Chamber of Deputies. This Chamber contains 99 seats: 53 are for Christians (30 Maronites, 11 Greek Orthodox, 6 Greek Catholic, 4 Armenian Orthodox, 1 Armenian Catholic, 1 Protestant), 39 are for Muslims, 6 for Druses and one other.

Area: 10,400km²; **Population:** 2,658,000 (1980); **Capital:** Beirut (population 1978, 702,000); **Other cities:** Tripoli (175,000); **Official language:** Arabic; **Adult literacy rate:** 72% (1977); **Health:** 8 doctors per 10,000 people; 4 hospital beds per 1000 people; **Average life expectancy at birth:** 65 years; **Unit of currency:** Lebanese pound; **Exports** (in order of value): precious metals, stones, jewellery and coins; vegetable products; non-precious metals and products; manufactured food and tobacco; **Imports** (in order of value): precious metals, stones, jewellery and coins; machinery and electrical apparatus; mineral products; textiles; **Per capita GNP:** US $1070 (1974).

Libya

LIBYA, Africa's fourth largest country, has been called the Socialist People's Libyan Arab Jamahiriya since 1977. (Jamahiriya means 'the State of the Masses'.)

THE LAND More then 90 per cent of Libya is in the Sahara which rises to Pico Bette, 2266 metres above sea level, in the south-east. The Sahara contains plateaux and vast depressions, in which such oases as Khufra, Marzuq and Sebha are situated. In the north the desert extends to the Mediterranean Sea along the Gulf of Sidra (Sirte), dividing the northern coastlands into two parts. The north-west contains a triangular lowland, 300-400km long and about 150km wide in the far north-west. This, Libya's most populous region, includes the capital Tripoli. It extends eastwards to a point between Homs and Misurata. This region, the Jefara, is bounded inland by a steep escarpment with several local names and generally called the Jabal. It rises to 968 metres near Gharian. South of the Jabal is a plateau which merges into the Sahara. The north-east contains a narrow

The graceful Sidi Beliman mosque in Tripoli. The Libyan Arabs practically without exception follow Sunni Muslim rites.

coastal plain backed by a limestone upland, called the Jabal Akhdar.

Libya has a hot, dry climate and there are no perennial streams. The average annual temperature range is 12°C-26°C at Tripoli and 14°C-27°C at Benghazi. The world's highest shade temperature, 58°C, was recorded at Al-Aziziyah in 1922. The rainfall varies from 330mm a year in Tripoli to 250mm in Benghazi and 500-600mm in the Jabal Akhdar. The Sahara has less than 125mm per year. In the north is Mediterranean scrub, wild esparto grass in the Jefara, woodlands on the uplands in the north-east and dry steppe merging into total desert in the south. Wildlife includes desert foxes, gazelles, jerboas, snakes and wildcats.

ECONOMY Since 1960 oil has dominated the economy and Libya is now Africa's second largest producer, having deliberately reduced production in the 1970s. The chief oilfields are in the Sahara, principally south and south-east of the Gulf of Sidra. Natural gas is also produced and there are deposits of iron ore, gypsum, salt and sulphur.

Farmland covers 1.5 per cent of Libya, pasture 3.8 per cent and woodland 0.3 per cent. Although it contributes only 2 per cent of the GDP, agriculture still employs 23 per cent of the workforce and the government is extending farmland through irrigation projects. The chief farm regions are the Jefara, particularly the Gharian-Tripoli-Homs triangle, the north-east where animal husbandry is most important, and the oases, which are dominated by date palms. The chief crops are barley, dates, fruits, groundnuts, olives, vegetables and wheat. In 1980 there were 6,000,000 sheep, 1,500,000 goats and 180,000 cattle. However, four-fifths of Libya's food is still imported. Manufacturing was traditionally small-scale, but many industries, especially petrochemical ones, are now growing.

The chief seaports are Tripoli, which also has the leading airport, Benghazi and the oil terminals of Marsa al-Brega, Es-Sider, Marsa al-Hariga (the port of Tobruk), Ras Lunf and Zuetina. There were 5173km of roads in 1978, the most important being the north coastal road linking the main towns. In 1978 Italy, West Germany, France, Japan and the UK were the major import suppliers, while the USA and Western Europe were the main markets for oil in 1977. But in the late 1970s relations with the USA deteriorated and, in 1981, the USA put an embargo on Libyan oil imports. Tourism is not important in Libya.

PEOPLE Most Libyans are of Arab or Berber origin, although there is a substantial foreign population (18 per cent of the total in 1973). Although thinly populated, the annual rate of population increase in Libya in 1970-79 was 4.2 per cent, which would double the population in only 17 years.

The proportion of people in urban areas has increased from 23 per cent in 1960 to 52 per cent in 1980, a consequence of the expansion of the economy in that period. Only 30 years ago, Libya was a poor country, but today its huge oil revenue is being used not only to develop and diversify the economy, but also to supply free education, medical services, care for the old, and housing for all. One daily newspaper is published and, in 1980, there were 131,000 radios and 160,000 television sets in circulation.

HISTORY From early times, Libya came under the influence of many cultures, including those of ancient Egypt, Phoenicia, Carthage and Greece. Rome occupied the north by AD 85 and in the 5th and 6th centuries there were periods of Vandal and Byzantine rule. The Arabs conquered Libya in 643 and most of the indigenous Berbers soon embraced Islam. From 1551 the north was part of the Ottoman Empire, but Italian rule began when Italy seized Tripoli in 1911. From 1943 Britain ruled the northern provinces of Tripolitania and Cyrenaica, while France governed the south-western province of Fezzan.

The fully independent United Kingdom of Libya (a federation of the three provinces) was established on December 24, 1951, under King Idris I. In 1963 Libya became a unitary state and, in 1969, the King was deposed and a republic was proclaimed. A Revolutionary Command Council, headed by Colonel Muammar al-Gaddafi, took control and the Senate and House of Representatives were abolished.

In 1973 a 'cultural revolution' was launched. People's committees were set up. They were dedicated to Arab nationalism and socialism, opposing 'capitalist materialism and communist atheism'. Libya has also recently pursued an increasingly forceful role in international affairs and has aided nationalist and revolutionary groups in several countries, such as Eritreans in Ethiopia, Muslim rebels in the Philippines and Muslim forces in neighbouring Chad. Libya's policies were criticised in several countries, particularly the USA. In 1981 US naval forces shot down two Libyan jet fighter planes in a clash in the Gulf of Sidra, whose waters are disputed, and in 1982 the USA announced trade sanctions against Libya.

GOVERNMENT Libya has a system of direct democracy, with 186 Basic and 46 Municipal People's Congresses at local level. Officials of these Congresses form the General People's Congress (the national legislature) and members of the GPC form a General People's Committee, which heads the government departments. Colonel Gaddafi, the Revolutionary Leader, is Head of State.

Area: 1,759,540km²; **Population:** 3,233,000 (1982); **Capital:** Tripoli (population 1973, 707,000); **Other cities:** Benghazi (332,000), Zawia (244,000), Misurata (178,000), Homs (161,000), Gharian (154,000); **Official language:** Arabic; **Adult literacy rate:** 45% (1977); **Health:** 11 doctors per 10,000 people; 5 hospital beds per 1000 people; **Average life expectancy at birth:** 55 years; **Unit of currency:** Libyan dinar; **Exports:** petroleum (94 per cent of the total in 1976-78); **Imports** (in order of value): machinery and transport equipment, manufactured goods, food and live animals; **Per capita GNP:** US $8640 (1980).

Mauritania

MAURITANIA, in north-western Africa, is officially called the Islamic Republic of Mauritania.

THE LAND Plains and low plateaux cover most of Mauritania. The north is desert, but the rainfall increases to the south to 100-300mm in the grass steppe of the Sahelian zone. But the rainfall is unreliable and the Sahelian drought of 1969-74 caused much suffering. In the far south in the Senegal River valley, the rainfall reaches 750mm a year. This is the most densely populated region.

A camel market at Atar in north-western Mauritania. Camels are vital beasts of burden in the northern desert region.

ECONOMY The traditional economy was based on nomadic pastoralism, crop growing in the south and fishing. But since 1963 iron ore mined at F'Dérik has transformed the economy. Mauritania has other minerals, including copper at Akjoujt, but production here ceased in 1978 after proving uneconomic. Arable land covers 0.2 per cent of the land. The main products are dates, fruit, gum arabic, millet, sorghum and vegetables. In 1980 there were 5,200,000 sheep, 2,600,000 goats, 1,200,000 cattle and 740,000 camels. The fishing industry is expanding but there is little manufacturing. Nouakchott and Nouadhibou contain the main ports and airports. Nouadhibou exports iron ore which arrives on the 650km-long railway from F'Dérik. In 1977 Mauritania had more than 6000km of roads. In the mid-1970s France and the UK were the chief trading partners.

PEOPLE About 75 per cent of the people are of Berber or Arab origin, and 25 per cent are Negroids who live in the south, but nearly all of the people are Muslims. In 1960, 97 per cent of the people lived in rural areas. But the Sahelian drought led many to seek refuge in townships and, by 1975, nearly a quarter of the population was in urban areas. Educational services have expanded since 1960, but 83 per cent of adults are still illiterate. In 1979 there were 30,000 radio receiving sets in circulation and there is also a television service.

HISTORY Mauritania became a French protectorate in 1903 and a colony in 1920, but full independence was achieved on November 28, 1960. Mauritania became a one-party state in 1964 and Arabic became an official language, alongside French, in 1968, an indication of the government's desire to associate the nation with the Arab world. Mauritania joined the Arab League in 1973.

In February 1976, Spain withdrew from neighbouring Western Sahara and, through a treaty with Spain and Morocco, Mauritania incorporated the southern part of the territory (88,667km²). But guerrillas belonging to Polisario (Popular Front for the Liberation of Saharan Territories) launched a war, with raids into Mauritania. In 1978 a military group took power and, in August 1979, Mauritania withdrew from Western Sahara and renounced its sovereignty. (See Western Sahara.)

GOVERNMENT Since 1979 Mauritania has been ruled by a Military Committee for National Salvation.

Area: 1,030,700km²; **Population:** 1,723,000 (1982); **Capital:** Nouakchott (population 1976, 134,000); **Official languages:** Arabic, French; **Adult literacy rate:** 17% (1977); **Health:** 1 doctor per 10,000 people; 0.4 hospital beds per 1000 people; **Average life expectancy at birth:** 42 years; **Unit of currency:** Ouguiya; **Exports** (in order of value): iron ore (80% of the total in 1974-76), fish; **Imports** (in order of value): food products, vehicles and parts, petroleum products; **Per capita GNP:** US $320 (1980).

Western Sahara

WESTERN SAHARA, formerly Spanish Sahara, covers 266,000 square kilometres in north-western Africa. Its capital until 1975 was El Aaiún (Laayoune). In 1975 Spain withdrew and Morocco took the northern two-thirds and Mauritania the southern third. Mauritania withdrew in 1979 and Morocco took over the south but the guerrilla war, begun in 1975, continued into the 1980s.

THE LAND Most of Western Sahara is low and flat. The climate is hot and arid and even coastal areas have an average annual rainfall of less than 50mm. Most of the land is barren desert, with patches of low-grade pasture.

The people of Western Sahara are mostly nomadic pastoralists who move between the patches of scanty grassland.

ECONOMY The economy was based on herding camels, sheep and goats, with some fishing, until 1963 when huge phosphate deposits were discovered at Bu Craa, south-east of El Aaiún. By 1975 exports of dry phosphates had reached 2.6 million tonnes, although production stopped after the start of the guerrilla war.

PEOPLE In the 1970s census the population was 76,425, of whom 22 per cent were foreigners. But this census has been disputed and claims are made that the population is closer to 750,000. The people are of Arab or Berber origin. There are 12 groups, the largest being the Reguibat and the Tenka.

HISTORY Mauritania became a Spanish colony in 1884 and a Spanish province in 1960. In 1967 Spain set up an assembly of tribal chiefs and community leaders called the Djemaa. But in 1973 a group of students founded the nationalist Popular Front for the Liberation of Saharan Territories (Polisario), which began guerrilla activities against Spain.

In 1974 Spain announced its intention to withdraw and hand Western Sahara over to a pro-Spanish regime. Morocco and Mauritania submitted claims to the territories to the International Court of Justice in 1975. The Court rejected both claims but a Moroccan civilian army entered Western Sahara in November. Spain signed an agreement on November 14 to cede power to Morocco and Mauritania, partitioning Western Sahara between them in 1976. The agreement was endorsed by the Djemaa but there was no referendum. Polisario proclaimed the country to be the Southern Arab Democratic Republic and, with Algerian support, launched a guerrilla war which they carried into southern Morocco and

Mauritania. Tired of the war, Mauritania withdrew in 1979 but Morocco then occupied the southern third. In 1982 representatives of the Polisario Saharan Arab Democratic Republic were admitted to membership of the Organization of African Unity, a step that seriously divided the Organization.

Morocco

MOROCCO is a constitutional monarchy in north-western Africa.

THE LAND Morocco is a complex region including the folded Atlas mountains, plateaux and plains. The rugged Rif Atlas in the north is separated from the Middle Atlas by the fertile Rharb-Sebou lowlands, the Taza gap and the Moulouya valley. South of the Middle Atlas is the High Atlas where Morocco's highest peak, Djebel Toubkal (4165 metres above sea level), is situated. In the south-west, the arid Souss plain separates the High Atlas from the Anti-Atlas, east of which the land slopes down to the Sahara. West of the Atlas ranges is the Meseta, a plateau averaging about 300 metres above sea level, and the narrow Atlantic coastal plain. The mostly low-lying Western Sahara is in the far south (see Western Sahara).

Northern Morocco has hot, dry summers and cool, moist winters: Tangier has an average annual rainfall of 810mm. In the interior, west- and north-facing mountain slopes have an average annual rainfall of 760mm a year, but east- and south-facing slopes are arid, although snow covers the highest peaks in winter. The rainfall generally decreases from north to south: Agadir has only 250mm a year. But the cool Canaries Current keeps down temperatures on the Atlantic coast.

The vegetation ranges from Mediterranean maquis in the north, to oak, cedar and pine forests on mountain slopes, steppe and scrub on drier uplands, and semi-desert and desert in the south and south-east.

ECONOMY Morocco is rich in mineral resources, though most are little exploited at present. The chief mineral is phosphate rock and Morocco is the third largest producer after the USA and the USSR. The incorporation of Western Sahara in 1976 has greatly increased Morocco's reserves, because of the large deposits at Bu Craa. Farmland covers 17 per cent of the land, pasture 28 per cent and woodland 12 per cent. Agriculture, forestry and fishing employ 55 per cent of the people. The main crops include barley, citrus fruits, olives, vegetables and wheat. In 1980 there were 16,100,000 sheep, 6,070,000 goats and 3,680,000 cattle. Sea fishing for anchovies, mackerel and sardines is also important. Major industries are

phosphate processing and oil refining. Other manufactures include processed foods, cement, chemicals and plastics and vehicles, as well as such traditional products as carpets, ceramics, leatherwork and textiles.

Casablanca, Safi and Mohammedia are major seaports and, in 1980, Morocco had 24,600km of surfaced roads and more than 1800km of railways. France is the chief trading partner. About 1.5 million tourists visit Morocco every year.

PEOPLE The population is increasing rapidly, by 3 per cent per year in 1970-79. Most people are Arabs, but about 35 per cent are Berbers who live mostly in mountain regions. Islam is the state religion and Arabic the official language, but Berber, French and Spanish are also spoken. In 1980 41 per cent of the population lived in urban areas, compared with 29 per cent in 1960. Education is compulsory between the ages of 7 and 13 and the radio and a special newspaper for the newly literate are used to combat the high rate of adult illiteracy. Four daily newspapers are published in Casablanca and five in Rabat. In 1978 about 2.4 million radio and 605,000 television sets were in circulation.

HISTORY In early times Morocco came under the influence of Phoenicians, Carthaginians and Romans. The Arabs took control of Morocco in the early 700s and in 711 Morocco was the starting point for the Muslim conquest of the Iberian peninsula.

European interest in Morocco mounted in the 19th century and in 1912 the territory was divided between France and Spain with an international zone at Tangier. In 1956 French and Spanish Morocco (except for the Spanish enclaves of Ceuta and Melilla) became independent. Tangier was restored

Agriculture is crucial to the economy of Morocco and a wide variety of crops thrive in the different climatic regions. Morocco is one of the world's largest exporters of citrus fruits.

to Morocco and lost its special status in 1959. In 1961 Hassan II succeeded to the throne on the death of his father Mohammed V.

Morocco was enlarged in 1969 when Spain handed over Ifni, a tiny enclave in the south-west. Morocco also claimed Spanish (now Western) Sahara to the south, arguing that it was part of Morocco in medieval times. In 1975 Spain, Morocco and Mauritania agreed that Western Sahara would be partitioned after Spain's withdrawal in February 1976. Morocco took the northern two-thirds, but the Popular Front for the Liberation of Saharan Territories (Polisario) proclaimed the territory to be the Saharan Arab Democratic Republic. With Algeria's support, Polisario began a guerrilla war. Mauritania's economy was severely weakened by the war and it withdrew from the southern third of Western Sahara in 1979. Morocco then took over the complete territory. But the war continued and, in 1982, the Organization of African Unity was seriously split when Polisario representatives were admitted to an OAU ministerial meeting.

GOVERNMENT The King is the supreme civil and religious authority. He appoints the Prime Minister and Cabinet and can dissolve Parliament which consists of the Chamber of Representatives. This Chamber contains 264 members, 176 of whom are directly elected to 6-year terms, while 88 are elected by an electoral college representing commune and municipal councils, professional organizations and trade unions.

Area: 446,550km² (not including Western Sahara); **Population:** 21,411,000 (1982); **Capital:** Rabat (population 1971, 436,000); **Other cities:** Casablanca (1,371,000), Marrakesh (330,000), Fès (321,000), Meknès (245,000), Tangier (186,000), Oujda (156,000); **Official language:** Arabic; **Adult literacy rate:** 28% (1977); **Health:** 1 doctor per 10,000 people; 1 hospital bed per 1000 people; **Average life expectancy at birth:** 55 years; **Unit of currency:** Dirham; **Exports** (in order of value): phosphates; food, drink and tobacco; phosphoric acid; carpets, clothing; **Imports** (in order of value): industrial equipment; semi-finished products; energy and lubricants; food, drink and tobacco; **Per capita GNP:** US $860 (1980).

Oman

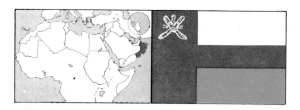

OMAN, a Sultanate on the eastern corner of the Arabian peninsula, was called the Sultanate of Muscat and Oman until 1970. Oman's borders have

not been precisely defined, but there is agreement on their general lines.

THE LAND Northern Oman contains a fertile coastal plain, called the Batinah, which lies north-west of Muscat. Behind the coastal plain is a rugged highland region, called the Jabal Akhdar, which rises to more than 3000 metres. Some wadis in the deeply dissected highlands contain springs and wells. Central Oman consists of a barren plateau that merges into the 'Empty Quarter' of Saudi Arabia. In the far south, the Dhufar coast near the Yemen PDR border is a fertile region. Oman also includes a small, mountainous area at the tip of the Musandam peninsula, which overlooks the strategically important Strait of Hormuz. This region, called the Ru'us al Jibal, is separated from the rest of Oman by part of the United Arab Emirates.

The climate is hot and arid. Muscat has an average annual temperature range of 21°C to 43°C and an average annual rainfall of only 100mm. The Jabal Akhdar is the best watered region, with about 250mm of rain per year, although some places have as much as 500mm. The Jabal Akhdar contains some pasture and irrigated wadis. Near the coast the increasing demand for fresh water has lowered the water table, causing seawater to seep into water-bearing rock layers. Water improvement projects are being developed to solve this problem.

ECONOMY Oman has the 7th highest per capita GNP in the Arab world. The economy is dominated by oil, the production of which began in 1967. Revenue from oil sales is being used to diversify the economy. Recent developments are the exploitation of natural gas, which was formerly flared off, and the mining of copper, chromite and other minerals. The government is also investing in the expansion of agriculture and fishing. Farming is currently limited to land around oases, but dates and other fruits, vegetables and some cereals are grown, although much food is imported. Pasture covers nearly 5 per cent of the land and, in 1980, Oman had 206,000 goats, 137,000 cattle and 79,000 sheep. Rich fishing grounds, containing crayfish, sardine and whitebait, lie offshore. There is little manufacturing, but the government is encouraging industrial development. Tourism is another industry with much unrealized potential.

Oman's leading port is Mina Qaboos and there are international airports at Seeb and Salalah. There are more than 12,000km of roads. Japan, Singapore, the Netherlands and West Germany are major customers for Oman's oil. Leading suppliers of imports include the UK, the United Arab Emirates and Japan.

PEOPLE About 90 per cent of the population is of Arab origin. There are also some descendants of black African slaves and immigrant workers from India, Iran, Pakistan and South Korea. Oman has never had a census, but World Bank data suggests that the population has been increasing in 1970-79 by 3.2 per cent per year, a rate that would double the population in only 22 years. Arabic is the official language, but English is also spoken.

Gas flares at a separator station at Fahud. The economy of Oman is dominated by oil.

Before the palace coup of 1970, Oman lacked social services. There was only one hospital, which was in Muscat, but by 1979 there were 13 hospitals spread throughout the country, increasing the number of hospital beds by more than a hundredfold. Oil revenue has also been used to expand the free but not compulsory educational facilities, particularly in the primary sector. In 1970 there were three schools in Oman with about 900 pupils, all of whom were boys. By 1979 Oman had 363 primary schools and almost 95,000 pupils, about one-third of whom were girls. However, secondary and higher education is still much more limited. Oman has one daily newspaper and there are radio and colour television services. In 1980 there were 35,000 television sets in circulation.

HISTORY In ancient times, Oman was a major Indian Ocean trading centre. In the 7th century, Oman became one of the first areas to embrace Islam. Portugal ruled the area from 1508 to 1648, when they were turned out by Imam Nasir bin Murshid. Oman's power steadily increased and, by 1730, it had taken all the Portuguese settlements in East Africa, including Zanzibar, which it held until the second half of the 19th century. But civil wars in Oman led to Iranian intervention. The Iranians were finally expelled by Ahmad bin Said, who was elected Imam in 1749, founding the Al Bu Said dynasty which still rules Oman.

In the 19th century, Oman made several treaties of friendship with European powers, including Britain. British influence increased and in 1891 a treaty put Oman under British protection. Between 1964 and 1975 left-wing guerrillas in Dhufar province, supported by the Yemen PDR, waged an armed revolt against the government, but the guerrillas were defeated in 1975 with the help of Iranian troops. In 1970 Sultan Qaboos bin Said deposed his father, who was an isolationist, and began a programme of reform and economic development. In 1971 Oman became fully independent and joined the Arab League and the United Nations. In 1980 Oman negotiated a defence alliance with the USA.

GOVERNMENT Oman is an absolute monarchy. The Sultan is Head of State, Prime Minister and Minister of Foreign Affairs, Defence and Finance.

Area: 212,457km^2; **Population:** 949,000 (1982); **Capital:** Muscat (population of Muscat and Matrah, 25,000); **Official language:** Arabic; **Adult literacy rate:** 20% (1977); **Health:** 5 doctors per 10,000 people; 2 hospital beds per 1000 people; **Average life expectancy at birth:** 48 years; **Unit of currency:** Rial Omani; **Exports:** petroleum (97% of the total in 1973-79); **Imports** (in order of value): machinery and transport equipment, manufactured goods, food and live animals; **Per capita GNP:** US $4380 (1980).

Palestine

Qatar

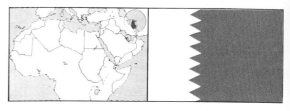

PALESTINE is a region bordering the south-eastern coast of the Mediterranean Sea. It was ruled by Britain from 1920 to 1948 as a League of Nations mandated territory. In 1948 the Jewish population of Palestine proclaimed part of Palestine to be the state if Israel, which sparked off the first Arab-Israeli war when Arab nations came to the assistance of the Palestinian Arabs.

By the end of the war, Israel controlled 20,770 square kilometres of Palestine, which had covered a total area of 27,090 square kilometres. Jordan took the area west of the Jordan River (Samaria and part of Judea, including part of the holy city of Jerusalem), which was called the West Bank (see Jordan). Another part of Palestine, the Gaza Strip in the south-west (area 378 sq km), became part of Egypt. However, in 1967, Israel occupied the West Bank, the Gaza Strip, part of Syria (the Golan Heights) and the Sinai peninsula of Egypt. The Sinai peninsula was returned to Egypt by April 1982 under the Egyptian-Israeli peace treaty of 1979.

Many Palestinian Arabs now live in exile in neighbouring Arab countries. From 1963 the Arab nations have recognized the Palestinian Liberation Organization as 'the sole legitimate representative of the Palestinian people'. The Arab League considers Palestine to be an independent state and, hence, a full member of the League, where it is represented by the PLO.

THE LAND There are four main land regions. The fertile coastal plain is widest in the south, but it narrows towards Haifa, where it is known as the Plain of Sharon. In the south the coastal plain becomes increasingly arid until it merges into the Sinai desert.

Inland are the limestone uplands of Galilee, Samaria and Judea. Galilee, in the north, contains the highest peak, Hare Meron, which is 1208 metres high. South of Nazareth is a large, fertile basin called the Emeq. South of the Emeq is Samaria, but the most rugged uplands are in Judea, which rises to 1020 metres north of Hebron.

The third region is the Rift Valley in the east. This extension of the great East African Rift Valley contains the Jordan River, Lake Tiberias (the Sea of Galilee), the Dead Sea, whose shoreline is the world's lowest point on land (393 metres below the level of the Mediterranean Sea), and the Gulf of Aqaba in the south.

The Negev, the fourth region, forms a triangle in the south, beyond the Beersheba basin. It extends to Elat on the Gulf of Aqaba. Irrigation has made parts of this desert region fertile.

The climate is characterized by hot, dry summers when temperatures soar to 32°C or more and mild, rainy winters. The floor of the Rift Valley is much hotter and extremely humid. About 1100mm of rain falls per year on the coast and 860mm on the interior uplands. The Negev is desert and Elat has an average of only about 30mm of rain per year. Snow may fall in Upper Galilee and Jerusalem.

QATAR is a Sheikdom occupying the Qatar peninsula and some small islands in the Arabian (Persian) Gulf. The peninsula is about 160km long and 55 to 80km wide.

THE LAND Apart from some low hills in the north-west, most of Qatar is flat and stony desert, with sand dunes and salt marshes in the south. The climate is hot and arid. In summer, temperatures often soar to 40°C and the humidity is usually high. Winters are relatively cool. The average annual rainfall is only about 130mm and supplies of underground water are limited, because much is too saline for drinking or for watering crops. Today more than half of Qatar's fresh water comes from desalination plants. The only area with any natural vegetation is in the north-west.

ECONOMY In comparatively recent times, Qatar's economy was based on fishing, pearl diving and some nomadic herding. By 1980, however, Qatar had the second highest per capita GNP in the Arab world after the United Arab Emirates. Qatar's new-found prosperity is based on oil and natural gas. Oil was first discovered in the 1930s and the export of oil began in 1949 after a pipeline had been laid from the Dukhan field in the east to the port of Umm Said in the west. In the early 1980s, it was estimated that the known oil reserves should last at least 35 years, while the offshore North Field contains what is probably one of the world's largest natural gas deposits.

Oil revenue has been used to diversify the economy. The fishing industry in the warm, shallow and fish-rich Gulf waters has been modernized and Doha has refrigeration and processing plants that prepare prawns for export. Agriculture is developing with government encouragement around wells and desalination plants, although farmland and pasture cover respectively only 0.4 and 4.5 per cent of the country. But Qatar is self-sufficient in vegetables, and fruits, especially dates, are important. In 1980 there were 48,000 goats, 42,000 sheep, 9000 camels and 7000 cattle but food must be imported. The government has also encouraged the growth of heavy industry, particularly at Umm Said. Qatar now has petrochemical, fuel and gas, fertilizer and iron and steel plants.

Doha has an international airport and its modern harbour was completed in 1969. In 1977 there were nearly 1500km of roads. Qatar's main trading partner is Japan.

PEOPLE Nearly all the people are Arabs and Arabic is the official language and Islam the state religion. But there are also some foreign workers and immigration

The Ras Abu Funtas power station completed in 1980 is part of a drive to develop industry and lessen Qatar's dependence on oil revenues.

in 1970-79 contributed to the extremely high annual rate of population increase of 7.6 per cent. Qatar is one of the world's most urbanized nations. Nearly 80 per cent of the people live in the capital Doha.

Qatar has devoted much of its oil revenue to social welfare. In 1945 there was only one hospital and one resident doctor, but Qatar's free medical services now compare favourably with other prosperous Arab nations. The government also provides allowances for the sick, the elderly, widows and orphans and low income families. Education is also free and the number of children at primary schools has increased from 1388 (all of whom were boys) in 1956, when state education was first introduced, to 25,000 (48 per cent girls) in 1980-81. Facilities for secondary education are more limited, but many scholarships are available for those who want to get higher education overseas. Qatar has several weekly and monthly publications and there are radio and colour television stations in Doha.

HISTORY Between 1872 and World War I Qatar was nominally under the control of the Ottoman Empire. In 1916 a treaty made Qatar a British protected state. This treaty remained in force until 1971 when Qatar became fully independent. It then joined the Arab League and the United Nations. HH Shaikh Kalifa bin Hamad Al-Thani, whose family has ruled Qatar since 1868, became Emir in 1972. He continued to modernize the country while also preserving the Islamic way of life.

GOVERNMENT The Emir is Head of State and he appoints the Council of Ministers in which executive power resides. There is also a 30-member Advisory Council, selected from representatives who are elected by a limited suffrage. Since 1975 this Advisory Council has had the power to question ministers on legislation before its promulgation.

Area: 11,000km²; **Population:** 267,000 (1982); **Capital:** Doha (population 1980, 180,000); **Official language:** Arabic; **Adult literacy rate:** 25% (1977); **Health:** 11 doctors per 10,000 people; 7 hospital beds per 1000 people; **Average life expectancy at birth:** 48 years; **Unit of currency:** Qatar Riyal; **Exports:** petroleum (96% of the total in 1973-80); **Imports** (in order of value): electrical equipment and apparatus, machinery and spares, transport equipment, food, textiles, clothing and footwear; **Per capita GNP:** US $26,080 (1980).

Saudi Arabia

SAUDI ARABIA occupies four-fifths of the Arabian peninsula.

THE LAND The Red Sea in the west is in a down-faulted trough that is structurally part of the East African Rift Valley system. Behind the narrow Red Sea coastal plain (the Tihama) is a range of mountains which are the uplifted rim of the ancient land mass that forms the Arabian peninsula. The mountains in the north, the Hijaz (Barrier), are particularly rugged, with many jagged lava flows. They reach heights of more than 2600 metres. South of the latitude of Medina, the mountains are lower, reaching about 1200 metres.

Here the Tihama is at its greatest extent, affording a corridor into the interior. South of Mecca, the land rises again in the Asir highlands, which contain Jebel Abha. At 3133 metres above sea level, this is Saudi Arabia's highest peak.

The Arabian peninsula tilts downwards to the north and east to the broad, oil-rich al-Hasa plain on the Gulf. Water-bearing rocks underlie the plain; the underground water originates far to the west. The interior of Saudi Arabia contains varied desert scenery. Both the Nefud in the north and the Rub al Khali in the south contain vast seas of sand, while the central Nejd has some large oases, including Riyadh.

The climate is hot and dry, although temperatures are modified by the altitude. The Red Sea coast is hot and humid. Jidda has an average annual temperature range of 22°C (January) to 30°C (July), while the average January temperature at Riyadh is 14°C. Large diurnal temperature ranges are experienced in the interior. The Asir highlands are the best watered region, with about 370mm of rain per year, as compared with only 80mm at Riyadh. Rain is rare in much of the interior. Saudi Arabia lacks perennial streams and barren desert covers most of the land.

Oil tanks, pipes and flares at Abqaiq, one of the world's largest oilfields. Saudi Arabia is by far the world's leading oil exporter and has controlled production to maintain stable oil prices.

Oases are centres of vegetation and the highlands contain some woodland and grassland.

ECONOMY Saudi Arabia is the world's leading oil exporter and, in 1980, its total output was exceeded only by that of the USSR. Saudi Arabia has the highest total GNP in the Arab world. Its per capita GNP increased in real terms by 9.6 per cent per year in 1970-79 and, by 1980, it was about the same as those of the USA and the Netherlands. Saudi Arabia also has the world's largest oil reserves, estimated at 26 per cent of the world total in the early 1980s.

Oil revenue is used to diversify the economy, particularly through massive five-year development plans. The 1975-80 plan gave emphasis to industrial and urban development, defence and education. The 1980-85 plan devoted more resources to agriculture, water desalination, irrigation and improvements in rural living conditions. Farmland accounts for only 0.5 per cent of the country and is concentrated around oases, wells and desalination plants. The chief crops include dates and other fruits, sorghum, wheat and vegetables. In 1980 there were 4 million sheep, about 2 million goats, 400,000 cattle and 156,000 camels. But agriculture accounts for only 1 per cent of the GDP (as compared with 76 per cent from industry and 23 per cent from services) and food makes up about one-tenth of the imports. Manufacturing is expanding rapidly, especially oil and gas refining.

Major international airports are at Jidda, Dhahran and Riyadh. Jidda and Dammam are the leading seaports. The main railway, which links Riyadh with Dammam, passes through the oilfields of the al-Hasa. Transport facilities are being increased under the five-year plans. By 1980 Saudi Arabia had about 21,000km of asphalted roads and 22,000km of dirt roads. The leading markets for exports are Japan, the USA, France and Italy. Import suppliers include the USA, West Germany, the UK and Italy. Saudi Arabia is a major aid donor to Arab and other developing nations. Between 1974 and 1980, an average of 827,000 Muslim pilgrims visited Saudi Arabia each year.

PEOPLE Nearly all the people are Arabs, although some people of Negroid ancestry live in the Red Sea region. Islam is the official religion and the basis of the country's laws. Saudi Arabia contains 1.5 to 2 million foreigners, two-thirds of whom are from the Arab world, one-fifth from other Asian nations, and the rest largely from Europe and the USA. In 1970-79 the population increased by the high annual rate of 4.6 per cent, which would double the population in 16 years. In 1980, 67 per cent of the people lived in urban areas, as compared with 30 per cent in 1960. The rural population is concentrated around oases, although some Bedouins still lead nomadic lives.

Oil revenue is also used to develop social welfare and the average life expectancy at birth has increased from 38 years in 1960 to 53 years in 1978. Education is free and adult education is being used to combat the high rate of illiteracy. There are 10 daily newspapers and, in 1980, there were 300,000 radio and 310,000 television receiving sets in circulation.

HISTORY Saudi Arabia, with its holy cities of Mecca and Medina, is the spiritual home of Islam. In the 7th century, it became the centre of a huge empire that, by the AD 730s, extended from Spain to India. From 1517 Saudi Arabia was part of the Ottoman Empire, but the Turks were driven out by the Arab Revolt in World War I. Modern Saudi Arabia was founded by Ibn Sa'ud who united the nation taking the title of King Hejaz in 1926 and King of Hejaz and its Dependencies in 1927. The name Saudi Arabia was adopted in 1932.

In 1945 Saudi Arabia joined the United Nations and the Arab League. It participated in the Arab-Israeli war in 1948 and it was also involved in later conflicts, giving aid to the front-line nations. King Ibn Sa'ud died in 1953 and was succeeded by King Sa'ud. Faisal ibn Abdul-Aziz became King in 1964, but he was assassinated in 1975 and Khalid ibn Abdul-Aziz became King. In the late 1970s and early 1980s, Saudi Arabia's importance in Arab and world affairs steadily increased. In 1981, Saudi Arabia, Bahrain, Kuwait, Oman, Qatar and the UAE set up the Gulf Co-operation Council, which was aimed at increasing economic co-operation.

GOVERNMENT The King is Head of State and Prime Minister. He is the focus of power and the supreme religious leader. He is assisted by a Council of Ministers. There are no elections and no political parties.

Area: 2,149,690km²; **Population:** 9,803,000 (1982); **Capital:** Riyadh (population 1974, 667,000); **Other cities:** Jidda (561,000), Mecca (367,000), Taif (205,000), Medina (198,000); **Official language:** Arabic; **Adult literacy rate:** 23% (1977); **Health:** 5 doctors per 10,000 people; 1 hospital bed per 1000 people; **Average life expectancy at birth:** 53 years; **Unit of currency:** Riyal; **Exports:** petroleum (about 99.7% of the total in 1976-78,; **Imports** (in order of value): machinery, metals and metal products, transport equipment, food; **Per capita GNP:** US $11,260 (1980).

Somalia

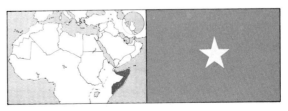

SOMALIA, in the Horn of Africa, is officially called the Somali Democratic Republic.

THE LAND Behind the generally narrow northern coastal plain bordering the Gulf of Aden are highlands. The highest point, 2406 metres above sea level, is in the Midjertine region, west of Erigavo. Central and southern Somalia consist of vast plateaux and plains that slope generally south-eastwards to the dune-lined Indian Ocean coast. The south contains Somalia's only two permanent rivers, the Shebele and Juba, both of which rise in Ethiopia.

The climate is hot and arid. In low-lying areas, average temperatures are between 27°C and 31°C, although the uplands are cooler. The northern coast is arid, many areas having less than 120mm of rain per year. More rain falls on the uplands and in the south. Mogadishu has an average annual rainfall of 400mm, while more than 500mm falls in the far south. However, the rainfall is everywhere unreliable and droughts are common. Large areas are semi-desert or dry savanna. Woodland is mostly confined to the highlands and the river valleys. South-western Somalia has a rich variety of wildlife, including antelopes, baboons, crocodiles, elephants, giraffes, hyenas, leopards, lions, monkeys, rhinoceroses, warthogs and zebras.

ECONOMY Prolonged droughts in the 1970s and the Somali-Ethiopian War of 1977-78 have disrupted the economy. Recent statistics are unavailable, but with a per capita GNP of US $130 in 1978, Somalia was the poorest nation in the Arab League. The country has limited but unexploited mineral resources. Livestock dominate the economy and, despite heavy losses in the 1970s, Somalia had 16,300,000 goats, 10,192,000 sheep, 5,450,000 camels and 3,900,000 cattle in 1980. Farmland covers less than 2 per cent of the land. The main farming regions are in and between the two southern rivers. Crops include bananas, citrus fruits, cotton, maize, sesame, sorghum, sugar-cane and vegetables. Frankincense and myrrh are collected in the northern uplands and ambergris along the coast. Fishing is increasing, but manufacturing, 80 per cent of which is government-owned, is small-scale, concerned with processing primary products and producing basic consumer goods.

Coastal shipping is important because internal transport is generally difficult. The chief port is Mogadishu. There are no railways, but the inadequate road network is being improved. Somalia has long suffered an adverse balance of trade and aid from Arab nations, the EEC, the USA and United Nations agencies is important. In the late 1970s the pattern of Somalia's trade changed as the country turned from the USSR to the West, but Saudi Arabia remains a major market for Somali exports. Tourism is un-important.

PEOPLE The Somalis are Hamites and their ancestors came from Arabia. There are also some Arabs, some Negroids, Europeans and Somali-speaking refugees from Ethiopia. By 1980 30 per cent of the people lived in urban areas. Most of the others were nomadic herdsmen. In Somalia the average life expectancy at birth is 43 years, which is one of the world's lowest rates. Health standards are aggravated by nutritional diseases; it was estimated that in 1981 the average daily calorie intake was only 80 per cent of the WHO required amount. The nomadic life style of many Somalis makes it difficult to bring effective health and educational services to the majority. Traditionally there has been a low literacy rate but a literacy drive was launched in 1975 and it proved successful

because many Somalis were confined to relief camps, a consequence of the severe drought. Also the number of pupils at school rose by five times and the university enrolment by 10 times in 1969-79. Somali and Arabic are the official languages and nearly all the people are Muslims. There are about 75,000 radio receivers in circulation and a television service is planned. The one daily newspaper is published in Mogadishu.

HISTORY In early times Somalia was called the Land of Spices. Arab influence was strong from the 10th century and, between the 13th and 16th centuries, there was conflict between Ethiopian Christians and Somali Muslims. After the opening of the Suez Canal in 1869, Somalia became strategically important. The north became a British protectorate in 1884-86 and Italy took over the south between 1889 and 1905. Frontier settlements split the Somali nation into five countries. Besides British and Italian Somalilands, there were also significant Somali populations in French Somaliland (Djibouti), Kenya and Ethiopia, a division that has led to a desire for a Greater Somalia that would reunite all Somalis.

In World War II Britain occupied Italian Somaliland, although Italian rule was restored in 1950 under a UN Trusteeship. In 1960 British Somaliland and Italian Somaliland became independent and they merged to form Somalia. In 1969 the armed forces seized control. General Mohammed Siad Barre, head of the ruling Supreme Revolutionary Council, became Head of State. In the early 1970s Somalia had close ties with the USSR, but relations deteriorated when the Russians supported Ethiopia in the Ogaden War of 1977-78, in which Somali troops aided the Western Somali Liberation Front which wanted to unite the Ethiopian Ogaden with Somalia. From 1978, Somalia turned increasingly to the non-communist world. A new Constitution was promulgated in 1979 and an Assembly was elected. But, in October 1980, a state of emergency was declared and the Supreme Revolutionary Council (suspended in 1976) was reconstituted.

GOVERNMENT The President is the chief executive and heads the Supreme Revolutionary Council. He is nominated by the Central Committee of the Somali Revolutionary Socialist Party, and is elected by the 127-member National Assembly, most of whose members are elected by universal suffrage.

Area: 637,657km²; **Population:** 4,096,000 (1982); **Capital:** Mogadishu (population 1980, 400,000); **Official languages:** Somali, Arabic; **Adult literacy rate:** 5% (1977); **Health:** 1 doctor per 10,000 people, 2 hospital beds per 1000 people; **Average expectancy at birth:** 48 years; **Unit of currency:** Somali shilling; **Exports** (in order of value): live animals, bananas, hides and skins; **Imports** (in order of value): manufactured goods, machinery and transport equipment, food and live animals, chemicals, fuels and lubricants; **Per capita GNP:** US $130 (1978).

Sudan

SUDAN, Africa's largest country, is officially called the Democratic Republic of the Sudan.

THE LAND Flat plains cover most of Sudan, which contains much of the upper sections of the White Nile, Blue Nile and Atbara river basins. Highlands include the Red Sea Hills, which reach 2259 metres at Jabal Oda in the north-east and the western Darfur Highlands which rise to 3088 metres at the volcanic Jabal Marra. Mountains in the far south include Mount Kinyeti near the Uganda border which, at 3187 metres, is Sudan's highest peak. The Nuba Mountains are the only uplands in central Sudan.

Sudan has a hot tropical climate. The north is particularly arid with less than 120mm of rain per year. Most people live in the Nile valley, which contains part of Lake Nasser. But desert and scrub cover most of the north. Central Sudan (16°N-10°N) contains the Darfur Highlands which receive about 760mm of rain per year, but most of this region is hot, semi-arid savanna. Irrigation is necessary for farming except in the Nuba Mountains where the rainfall is above average. The mountains of southern Sudan have an average annual rainfall of 1520mm and tropical forest grows there, with woodland on the south-eastern plateaux. After heavy rains, much of the upper White Nile valley, the *sudd*, is flooded and covered by masses of floating swamp plants. The southern Sudan is rich in wildlife and the Dinder National Park has much tourist potential.

ECONOMY Sudan is one of the Arab World's poorer nations. In 1980 its total GNP was about the same as that of Tunisia, but Tunisia's per capita GNP was three times larger than that of Sudan. Mining is unimportant and agriculture dominates the economy, although only five per cent of the land is farmed. Cotton and cotton products make up more than half of the exports, the chief cotton region being the Gezira district between the Blue and White Nile rivers south of Khartoum. Groundnuts, gum arabic and sesame are also important, while sorghum is the staple food crop. Sudan's cultivated area could be increased substantially and, with Arab aid for irrigation projects, Sudan hopes to become the 'breadbasket' of the Arab world. Nomadic pastoralism is also important and, in 1980, there were 18,354,000 cattle, 17,800,000 sheep, 12,570,000 goats and 2,500,000 camels. Manufacturing is concerned mainly with processing agricultural products and import substitution.

The only seaport, Port Sudan on the Red Sea, is

The Mahdi's tomb at Omdurman. The Mahdi, Muhammad Ahmad, led a rebellion against Egyptian and British forces from 1881 to 1888.

linked by rail to the Nile valley and most of the main cities. There is also a railway from Sennar to the west and south-west along which there has been substantial economic development. The road network is inadequate but it is being extended. The total length of river used for transport is about 4000km, 43 per cent of which is navigable throughout the year. In 1975 leading import suppliers were the UK, Japan, the USA and West Germany. Italy, France, China and Egypt were major export markets. There were large balance of trade deficits in the 1970s and these caused severe economic problems in the early 1980s.

PEOPLE Sudan is thinly populated, Khartoum and Blue Nile provinces being the most populous areas. In 1970-79 the population increased annually by an average of 2.7 per cent and, in 1980, 25 per cent of the people lived in urban areas, as compared with 10 per cent in 1960. In the north most people are of Arab origin, some of whom are mixed with Hamites and Negroes. Islam is the main religion. In the south live Nilotes, such as Anuak, Dinka, Nuer and Shilluk, Nilo-Hamites and Negroid people, including the Azande. Traditional religions and Christianity predominate in the south. The cultural differences between North and South led to a civil war in 1964-72. About 115 languages are spoken in Sudan, with Arabic as the official language.

The government has been working to improve health and educational services, particularly to reduce the high illiteracy rate. In 1978 there were 1,135,000 radio and 95,000 television receiving sets in circulation. Two daily newspapers are published in Khartoum.

HISTORY Nubia and Kush were important early civilizations in northern Sudan. Christianity was introduced into the Nile region in AD 543-569 and it survived there until the 14th century. In 1820 Egypt installed a governor at Khartoum and the Egyptian Khedive Ismail appointed the Briton General Gordon as governor-general in 1877-79. In 1881 Muhammad Ahmad, called the Mahdi ('divine guide'), began a rebellion against Egyptian rule. Gordon returned in 1884 as governor-general but he died when Khartoum fell to the Mahdi in 1885. The rebellion ended in 1888 and, in 1889, Britain and Egypt agreed to rule Sudan jointly as a condominium.

Independence was achieved on January 1, 1956. A military coup in 1958 brought General Ibrahim Abboud to power, but civilian rule was restored in 1964. In 1969 a second military coup occurred and General Gaafar Mohammed Nimeri became President. In 1972 Nimeri ended the North-South civil war by granting the South regional autonomy. In the late 1970s declining exports, increasing imports and mounting inflation caused the economy to deteriorate and strict economic measures in 1981, involving price rises, caused some discontent in 1982.

GOVERNMENT Executive power is vested in the President, who is the nominee of the only political party, the Arab Socialist Union. The People's Assembly contains 304 members, 274 of whom are elected by universal adult suffrage and 30 of whom are nomin-

ated. The South has an elected 60-member Assembly, situated at Juba.

> **Area:** 2,505,813km²; **Population:** 19,376,000 (1982); **Capital:** Khartoum (population 1973, 334,000); **Other cities:** Omdurman (299,000), Khartoum North (151,000), Port Sudan (133,000); **Official language:** Arabic; **Adult literacy rate:** 20% (1977); **Health:** 1 doctor per 10,000 people; 1 hospital bed per 1000 people; **Average life expectancy at birth:** 46 years; **Unit of currency:** Sudanese pound; **Exports:** (in order of value): cotton and cotton products, gum arabic, groundnuts and groundnut products, sorghum; **Imports** (in order of value): machinery and transport equipment, petroleum products, metal manufactures; **Per capita GNP:** US $470 (1980).

Syria

SYRIA is officially called the Syrian Arab Republic.

THE LAND Behind the narrow Mediterranean coastal plain is the Ansariya range which rises to about 1500 metres. East of this range is the Orontes River valley. Syria's chief highlands are the Anti-Lebanon Mountains which reach 2814 metres at Mount Hermon on the Lebanese border in the south-west. East of the Orontes (Al Ghab) basin and the Anti-Lebanon Mountains are broad plateaux that descend in the north-east to the Euphrates River basin.

The western regions have a Mediterranean climate, with an average annual temperature range of 8°-32°C and an average annual rainfall of 940mm, with snow on the mountains in winter. To the east it becomes hotter and more arid and about three-fifths of the country has less than 250mm of rain per year. The vegetation includes coniferous forest in the highlands, Mediterranean maquis and desert scrub. Syria's wildlife includes deer, gazelles, wildcats, wolves and a variety of birds.

ECONOMY Syria's economy has traditionally been based on agriculture and trading, but industry has recently played an increasingly important part, accounting for 28 per cent of the GDP in 1978 as compared with 20 per cent from agriculture, forestry and fishing. The country's resources include oil, the leading export since 1974, natural gas and phosphates. Syria produced 8.5 million tonnes of oil in 1980, or about one-sixteenth of the output in neighbouring Iraq.

Arable land covers about 31 per cent of the land, pasture of varying quality 45 per cent and forests 2.5 per cent. The farmland is concentrated in the coastal

The famous water wheels at Hama on the River Orontes were used for irrigation in the Middle Ages. The lack of large scale irrigation schemes has resulted in widely fluctuating crop yields.

plain, the Orontes basin and the north-east, particularly in the river valleys and the Jazirah, east of the Euphrates River. Barley and wheat grow on about 44 per cent of the arable land and fruits, olives, sugar beet, tobacco and vegetables are also important. Cotton is the chief cash crop. In 1980 Syria had 8,800,000 sheep, 1,000,000 goats and 770,000 cattle. The most important manufactures are oil products, phosphates and textiles, although cement, steel and other industries are increasing rapidly.

Damascus has an international airport and Latakia is the chief seaport. In 1980 Syria had 7300km of surfaced roads. The railway network is being extended. Oil pipelines from Iraq provide an important source of foreign exchange in normal times. The value of Syria's exports increased greatly in recent years, but there are still large adverse trade balances. In 1980 major suppliers of imports included Iraq, West Germany, Italy and the USA, while major export markets were Italy, West Germany, the USSR and the USA. Tourism is important when political conditions permit. There were 1.27 million tourists in 1979, three-fifths of whom were from Jordan and Lebanon.

PEOPLE The population increased rapidly in 1970-79 by the high annual rate of 3.6 per cent, which would double the population in 20 years if it continued. There has also been a marked expansion of the

Health standards are rising and the average life expectancy at birth increased from 48 years in 1960 to 57 in 1978. There is free and compulsory education for 6-14 year olds. Syria has six daily newspapers and, in 1978, there were 2,230,000 radio and 461,000 television receiving sets in circulation.
urban population from 37 per cent in 1960 to 50 per cent in 1980 and shanty towns have developed around such cities as Damascus and Aleppo (Halab). About 90 per cent of the people are Arabs and Arabic is the official language. Minorities include the Kurds in the north (6 per cent), Turks and Palestinian refugees. About 88 per cent of the people are Muslims. Most of the rest are Christians and there are some Druses.

HISTORY The Syrian coast was part of the great trading civilization of Phoenicia in early times. But, throughout much of its history, syria was under foreign domination. The Arabs conquered Syria between AD 634 and 636 and, under the Umayyad dynasty, Damascus became the centre of a brilliant Arab empire that stretched from the Atlantic Ocean to India. In 750, however, the empire's capital was moved to Iraq by the Abbasid dynasty and Syria declined. From 1095-1291 Syria featured in Crusader wars and from 1516 Syria was part of the Ottoman Empire.

In 1920, despite nationalist demands for freedom, France began to rule Syria under a League of Nations mandate. An independent republic was proclaimed in 1941, although foreign troops remained in Syria until 1946. The early years of independence were marked by political instability. In 1948 Syria was involved in the Arab-Israeli War. In 1958 Syria joined Egypt and Yemen in the United Arab Republic, but it withdrew in 1961. In 1967 Israel seized part of Syria east and north of Lake Tiberias (the Golan Heights region). In 1970 General Hafiz al-Assad, former Defence Minister, took power and he was elected President in 1971. In 1973 there was further fighting in the Golan area and, in 1976, Syrian troops were sent to restore order in Lebanon. They remained there constituting the bulk of the Arab Deterrent Force. In 1980 Syria signed a Treaty of Friendship and Co-operation with the USSR.

GOVERNMENT Under the 1973 Constitution, Syria is a 'socialist popular democracy'. The President heads the government which he appoints. Legislative power is vested in the 195-member People's Council, which is elected by universal adult suffrage. There are five political parties grouped in the national Progressive Front, the dominant party being the Baath Arab Socialist Party.

Area: 185,180km²; **Population:** 9,635,000 (1982); **Capital:** Damascus (population with suburbs 1970, 923,000); **Other cities:** Aleppo (Halab, 639,000), Homs (215,000); **Official language:** Arabic; **Adult literacy rate:** 53% (1977); **Health:** 4 doctors per 10,000 people; 1 hospital bed per 1000 people; **Average life expectancy at birth:** 57 years; **Unit of currency:** Syrian pound; **Exports** (in order of value): petroleum (64% of the total in 1977-80), cotton and other textiles, fruit and vegetables; **Imports** (in order of value): mineral fuels and oils; metals and metal manufactures; cereals, fruit and vegetables; **Per capita GNP:** US $1340 (1980).

Tunisia

TUNISIA is the smallest country in North Africa.

THE LAND Northern Tunisia is a complex region, consisting of the easternmost part of the Atlas Mountains, including the northern Tell, the fertile Medjerda valley, and the High Tell (or Dorsale, meaning 'backbone'), which contains Tunisia's highest peak, Djebel Chambi, which is 1544 metres above sea level. Central Tunisia contains steppes in the west which slope eastwards to the broad coastal

plain, called the Sahel, which is dominated by olive tree cultivation. Southern Tunisia includes large salt lake depressions, the largest of which is Chott Djerid, which is 16 metres below sea level. Beyond these depressions are the Saharan plateaux of southern Tunisia.

The north has an average annual temperature range of 10°C to 27°C and an average annual rainfall of between 400 and 1000mm, although some mountain areas have more than 1500mm. As in other Mediterranean lands, most rain falls in winter. The rainfall decreases southwards to 200mm per year at Sfax and 180mm at Gabès. Mediterranean maquis and inland forests, with cork and evergreen oak, grow in the north, while central Tunisia is semi-arid grassland, merging into semi-desert and total desert in the south.

ECONOMY Tunisia's most important resources are minerals, notably oil and phosphates. In 1980 Tunisia produced 5.2 million tonnes of oil and was Africa's seventh largest producer. It was also the world's fifth largest phosphate producer in 1977. Tunisia also produces natural gas, iron ore, lead, zinc and other minerals.

Agriculture remains important and farmland covers about 32 per cent of the country, pasture 16 per cent and forests 3 per cent. The chief food crops are barley and wheat, while olive oil is the leading agricultural export. Other cereals, various fruits and vegetables are also grown. The chief farming districts are the northern mountain valleys, the north-east including the Cape Bon promontory, the Sahel and the central steppes, a grazing area. The only agriculture in the south is at oases, such as Tozeur near the Chott Djerid. The fishing industry employs more than 22,000 Tunisians and crayfish, mackerel, sardine, tunny and sponges are major products. Traditional craft industries remain important, but oil refining, phosphate manufacturing and other industries based on local minerals have been increasing. Tunis is the chief industrial centre. It has two airports and is the leading port, followed by Bizerta, Sousse and Sfax, the chief fishing port.

Transport facilities are best developed in the north. There are more than 21,000km of roads and, in 1978, there were 2257km of railways. Tunisia's imports consistently exceed the exports in value, producing marked unfavourable balances of trade. These are offset by remittances from Tunisian workers employed abroad, mainly in France, and by tourism which was the largest foreign exchange earner until it was overtaken by oil in 1976. Tunisia's tourist industry has expanded enormously in the last 20 years. In 1979 1,356,000 tourists visited Tunisia and the government hopes to increase the number to 2,200,000 by 1986. France is Tunisia's leading trading partner, followed by Italy, West Germany and Greece.

PEOPLE Most people are Arabs although there are also some Berbers, most of whom live in the south. The most densely populated areas are in the north, particularly the coastal cities and towns. In 1980 52 per cent of the people lived in urban areas, compared with 36 per cent in 1960. In 1970-79 the population increased by 2.1 per cent per year.

Health facilities are increasing and Tunisia has a better developed educational system than most developing nations, with free education from primary to university level. There are five daily newspapers, three in French, a language widely used in the higher grades of education, and two in Arabic. In 1980 there were 1,000,000 radio and 256,000 television sets in circulation.

HISTORY The Phoenicians established colonies in Tunisia, notably Carthage (just north of modern Tunis)

prices and unemployment caused unrest, particularly in the cities.

GOVERNMENT The Consitution of 1959 provides for an executive President who makes civil and military appointments. The National Assembly is elected to 5-year terms by universal adult suffrage. The Destour (Constitution) Socialist Party, led by Bourguiba, has dominated Tunisian politics since independence. In November 1981 Tunisia held its first multi-party elections for 22 years. The National Front, comprising the Destour Socialist Party and the General Union of

Kairouan is famous for its hand-woven carpets, but the traditional craft industries are giving way to industries based on local minerals.

in 814 BC. Carthage rose in might as Phoenicia declined and Carthage challenged the Roman Empire in the Punic Wars of 264-241 BC, 218-201 BC and 149-146 BC. In 146 the Romans razed Carthage to the ground, although they later rebuilt it. Arabs conquered Tunisia in AD 647, founding the holy city of Kairouan in 670. Tunisia became part of the Ottoman Empire in 1574 but, in 1881, France invaded the country and proclaimed it a protectorate.

After World War II, mounting nationalist opposition to French rule was manifested in guerrilla warfare in the early 1950s. Tunisia achieved independence on March 20, 1956 as a monarchy. In 1957, however, the Bey of Tunis was deposed and a republic proclaimed, with Habib Bourguiba, the prime minister, being elected President by the Constituent Assembly. Bourguiba was re-elected in 1959, 1964 and 1969. In 1974 he was elected President for life. In the late 1970s, despite the expansion of the economy, rising

Tunisian Workers (UGTT), decisively defeated the three opposition parties by winning 94.6 per cent of the votes cast.

Area: 163,610km²; **Population:** 6,624,000 (1982); **Capital:** Tunis (population 1975, 550,000); **Other cities:** Sfax (171,000); **Official language:** Arabic; **Adult literacy rate:** 55% (1977); **Health:** 2 doctors per 10,000 people; 2 hospital beds per 1000 people; **Average life expectancy at birth:** 57 years; **Unit of currency:** Dinar; **Exports** (in order of value): petroleum (41% of the total in 1976-79); phosphates, phosphoric acid and superphosphates; clothing; olive oil; **Imports** (in order of value): machinery; petroleum and petroleum products; iron and steel; wheat, vehicles; **Per capita GNP:** US $1310 (1980).

United Arab Emirates

UNITED ARAB EMIRATES, formerly the Trucial States, is a federation of seven sheikhdoms which are, in order of size, Abu Dhabi, Dubai, Sharjah, Ras al-Khaimah, Fujairah, Umm al-Quwain and Ajman.

THE LAND The UAE has two coastlines. The one on the Arabian (Persian) Gulf is lined in places by coral reefs, islands and salt marshes, while the other, shorter coastline is on the eastern side of the Musandam peninsula which the UAE shares with Oman. The western interior is mostly flat and merges in the south into the Empty Quarter of Saudi Arabia, but uplands in the Musandam peninsula reach a height of 2081 metres. Temperatures average 18°C in January but temperatures of 40°C are common in summer. The average annual rainfall is about 130mm, although the uplands are somewhat wetter and cooler. Most of the UAE is barren desert.

ECONOMY Before 1960 the country was one of the poorest in the Arab world, the chief activities being fishing, oasis farming, nomadic pastoralism and entrepôt trade in Dubai. Commercial production of oil began in 1962 and, by 1980, the UAE had the world's highest per capita GNP of US $30,070. The UAE is the Arab world's fourth largest oil producer, after Saudi Arabia, Iraq and Kuwait. In 1980 oil production totalled 82,980,000 tonnes, 78.3 per cent of which came from Abu Dhabi, 21.1 per cent from Dubai, and 0.6 per cent from Sharjah. Revenue from oil sales has been used to develop transport facilities, to diversify the economy, to provide welfare, to supply aid to Arab and other countries, and to make foreign investments, including the provision of capital for the World Bank and the IMF.

Only 12,000 hectares are used for growing crops, while another 200,000 hectares (2.4 per cent of the country) are classed as pasture. Dates, various fruits and vegetables are grown at oases, such as Al'Ain. In 1980 there were 280,000 goats, 120,000 sheep, 49,000 camels and 24,000 cattle. Food is imported. Although the number of fishermen declined from 6545 to 3955 in 1972-78, the catch increased by more than 50 per cent. Industry is mainly concerned with oil and gas extraction and construction, although there is a steel mill, cement factories and an aluminium plant. The small size of the local workforce hinders industrial development.

Great progress has been made recently in increasing transport facilities. There were no paved roads in 1960, but roads now link the capitals of the sheikhdoms. Japan, the UK, the USA and West Germany are major trading partners.

Traditional dhow building in Dubai. Before oil production began in 1962 trade and fishing were the main activities. Today the U.A.E. has the world's highest per capita GNP.

PEOPLE Most people are Arabs, but the proportion of expatriates has increased, according to some estimates, to 85 per cent of the population in 1982, as compared with 10 per cent in 1968. Immigration is largely responsible for the exceptionally high annual rate of population increase of 14.2 per cent in 1970-79. Most expatriates are from Arab countries. There are also Indians, Iranians, Pakistanis and Filipinos, with some Europeans and Americans.

There are elaborate welfare services and free medical treatment for all. Educational facilities have rapidly expanded at all levels. The number of pupils increased from 28,000 in 1971 to 124,000 in 1980. There are adult education centres to combat the high rate of illiteracy and a university was opened at Al'Ain in 1977. There are a number of daily, weekly and monthly publications in Arabic and English and, in 1980, 200,000 radio and 100,000 television receiving sets were in circulation.

HISTORY From the early 17th century, Arab and European pirates were active in the area and what is now the UAE was known as the Pirate Coast. In 1820 Britain concluded a General Treaty for Peace with local rulers aimed at suppressing piracy and the slave trade. This was followed by the Perpetual Maritime Treaty of 1853 which ensured British protection against outside attack, and the Exclusive Agreement of 1892, whereby Britain assumed responsibility for the sheikhdoms' foreign affairs and defence, while the rulers agreed not to cede territory or enter into treaties with any other foreign power.

Britain withdrew in 1971 and the United Arab Emirates was formed on December 2. In the 1970s moves were made to unify services between the sheikhdoms and to combine the defence forces. In foreign affairs, the UAE supported the Arab cause in the 1973 Arab-Israeli War and participated in Arab oil cut-backs and boycotts. In 1981 the UAE became a founder member of the Gulf Co-operation Council, together with Bahrain, Kuwait, Oman, Qatar and Saudi Arabia.

GOVERNMENT The UAE is headed by the Supreme Council, which consists of the seven rulers. The Council elects a President and Vice-President, who appoint the Council of Ministers. The Federal National Council, containing 40 members appointed by the seven sheikhdoms, has no specific powers, but it can propose amendments to new legislation and budget proposals.

Area: 83,600km²; Population: 1,161,000 (1982); Capital: Abu Dhabi (population 1978, 250,000); Official language: Arabic; Adult literacy rate: 25% (1977); Health: 41 doctors per 10,000 people; 85 hospital beds per 1000 people; Average life expectancy at birth: 48 years; Unit of currency: Dirham; Exports: petroleum (95% of the total in 1976-79); Imports (in order of value): manufactured goods, machinery and transport equipment, food and live animals, mineral fuels and lubricants; Per capita GNP: US $30,070 (1980).

North Yemen

YEMEN ARAB REPUBLIC is in the south-western corner of the Arabian peninsula.

THE LAND The plain bordering the Red Sea (the Tihama) is 30 to 80km wide. Inland are highlands that reach 3760 metres above sea level at Hadur Shu'ayb. In the east the land slopes down towards Saudi Arabia. The coast is hot and arid, with an average annual rainfall of about 130mm. The highlands, however, have up to 900mm of rain per year. The coastal plain is largely desert and the main farming regions are between 1400 and 2300 metres above sea level. Higher still are forests and grassland.

ECONOMY The country lacks minerals and has a lower per capita GNP than any other nation in the Arabian peninsula. Farmland occupies 15 per cent of the land, pasture 36 per cent and forests 8 per cent. Agriculture dominates the economy, employing 77 per cent of the labour force. The chief crops are cereals, fruits, vegetables, cotton (the leading export), qat (a narcotic), dates, tobacco and coffee. There are 7.3 million goats, 3.2 million sheep and nearly 1 million cattle. Textiles are the leading manufactures.

In recent years, the country has received substantial aid from Arab and other nations. The leading seaport is Hodeida, and Hodeida, Sana'a and Taiz have major airports. There are 1650km of roads. Saudi Arabia is the country's leading trading partner.

PEOPLE The Yemen Arab Republic is the most populous nation in the Arabian peninsula after Saudi Arabia. About 90 per cent of the population lives in rural areas. Many people work abroad. There were nearly 1.4 million emigrant workers in 1975, mostly in Saudi Arabia and other Gulf states. The country lags behind most of the Arab world in social services. A national television network was established by 1980 and an estimated 250,000 radio receivers were in circulation. There are two daily newspapers.

HISTORY In classical times, the region was part of an important trading region called Arabia Felix by the Romans. One famous kingdom in the area was that of Saba (or Sheba), which lasted from 950 to 115 BC.

The Ottoman Empire conquered the area in 1517, but its authority was frequently contested until the second half of the 19th century. The country became an independent monarchy in 1918. In 1962 the monarchy was overthrown by army officers who proclaimed the country a republic. A civil war then ensued until 1969. In the 1970s there was border conflict with the Yemen PDR, but the countries agreed

With many unique scenic and architectural features, the Yemen Arab Republic is attracting a growing tourist trade.

to unite in 1979. A draft Constitution was prepared by the end of 1981, but no date was announced for the merger.

GOVERNMENT The legislative body is the 159-member Constituent People's Assembly, which was appointed in 1978 to replace the military Command Council. The Cabinet is the executive body.

Area: 195,000km²; **Population:** 6,142,000 (1982); **Capital:** Sana'a (population 1980, 278,000); **Other cities:** Hodeida (126,000), Taiz (120,000); **Official language:** Arabic; **Adult literacy rate:** 13% (1977); **Health:** 1 doctor per 10,000 people; 1 hospital bed per 1000 people; **Average life expectancy at birth:** 47 years; **Unit of currency:** Riyal; **Exports** (in order of value): cotton, coffee, hides and skins; **Imports** (in order of value): machinery and transport equipment, manufactured goods, food and live animals; **Per capita GNP:** US $460 (1980).

South Yemen

YEMEN, PEOPLE'S DEMOCRATIC REPUBLIC OF is in the south-western part of the Arabian peninsula. It consists of the former territories of Aden, Aden Protectorate and the 17 former sultanates and emirates that constituted the Federation of South Arabia.

THE LAND Behind the generally narrow coastal plain, most of yemen is mountainous, occupying the up-tilted rim of the Arabian peninsula. The highest point is 2469 metres above sea level. Within the mountains is the broad, 640km-long Hadhramaut valley, an important farming region. In the north-east, the land descends to the Empty Quarter of Saudi Arabia.

Aden has an average annual temperature range of 24°C to 32°C and an average annual rainfall of 130mm. Some highland areas and the Hadhramaut get 760mm, but the eastern lowlands are arid for several years in succession. Most of Yemen is desert, although there is some grazing land.

ECONOMY Yemen lacks minerals and, outside the city of Aden, agriculture is the main activity, although farmland covers less than one per cent of the country. The chief food crops are barley, millet, sesame, sorghum and wheat, and cotton is the chief cash crop. In 1980 there were 1,350,000 goats, 380,000 sheep, 120,000 cattle and 100,000 camels. Fishing is important and fish made up more than a third of the exports in 1977. There is some light industry, but Aden's oil refinery, which processes imported oil, is the most important industrial enterprise. Transit trade is a major source of income in Aden, the chief seaport. Transport facilities inland are generally inadequate. Important trading partners include the UK and Japan, but aid, particularly from Arab and Communist nations, is important in sustaining the economy.

PEOPLE Most people are Arabs, although there are some North Yemenis, Indians, Pakistanis and Somalis. In 1980 37 per cent of the people lived in urban areas, as compared with 28 per cent in 1960. Yemen is a poor country — only Somalia and Mauritania in the Arab world have lower per capita GNPs. But the government is steadily increasing educational facilities, especially at primary level, which is free. There is one daily newspaper and about 150,000 radio and 25,000 television sets are in circulation.

HISTORY Britain annexed Aden in 1839 and the port became important after the opening of the Suez Canal in 1869. In 1882-1914 Britain established the Aden Protectorate.

After clashes between nationalist guerrillas and British troops, independence was achieved in 1967. The country's economy was severely hit by the closure of the Suez Canal (1967-75), and the subsequent loss in transit trade, but the economy began to recover in the late 1970s. Border disputes, especially with the Yemen Arab Republic, have caused problems, but the two Yemens agreed to unite in 1979. A draft Constitution was prepared by the end of 1981, but no date was announced for the proposed merger.

GOVERNMENT Under the amended 1978 Constitution, there is an elected 111-member Supreme People's Assembly. This Assembly appoints a 5-man Presidium, whose Chairman is the Head of State. The only party is the Yemen Socialist Party.

Area: 332,968km²; **Population:** 1,995,000 (1982); **Capital:** Aden (population 1973, 264,000); **Official languages:** Arabic; **Adult literacy rate:** 27% (1977); **Health:** 1 doctor per 10,000 people; 1 hospital bed per 1000 people; **Average life expectancy at birth:** 47 years; **Unit of currency:** Dinar; **Exports** (in order of value): food and live animals, petroleum products, cotton lint and seed; **Imports** (in order of value): machinery and transport equipment, food and live animals, petroleum products; **Per capita GNP:** US $420 (1980).

With an arid climate and few natural resources, the People's Democratic Republic of Yemen is amongst the poorest of the Arab nations.

Notes

Map 1 The Arab Nations

In theory there is only one Arab nation, and 21 Arab countries, including Palestine. For the purpose of this atlas, the area considered corresponds to the boundaries of those states which are members of the Arab League. This definition therefore excludes certain areas where Arabs form a majority of the population and includes other areas where Arabs are a minority.

The bonds which link Arab states are linguistic, religious and cultural rather than political. Serious differences of opinion on most of the major political issues of the day, including direct territorial disputes such as the Iran-Iraq war, have served to fragment the Arab world and, in effect, damage its unity and sense of a common purpose. The need to recognise and fulfil Palestinian aspirations for a state of their own has focussed Arab unity, though differences of approach remain, even on this issue. The Arab League itself has provided a valuable forum for discussing both internal matters of importance to the Arab world itself and external questions of policy affecting relations with the wider international community.

Map 2 The Shape of the Land

The greater part of the Arab lands is taken up by the ancient plateaux of northern Africa and Arabia, with narrow coastal plains backed nearly everywhere by steeply rising ground. The most notable mountains are the young fold ranges in north-western Africa which are prone to earthquakes. The most dramatic geological feature of the region is the great Rift Valley which runs south from Syria and includes the Dead Sea and the Red Sea. The shoreline of the Dead Sea is 393 metres below sea level, the world's lowest exposed land depression. Another striking feature is the paucity of rivers. There are only two major river systems in the entire region, the Nile and the Tigris/Euphrates. Internal drainage is a feature of much of northern Africa.

Map 3 Temperature and Insolation

The Arab lands are among the hottest in the world. The highest shade temperature ever recorded, 57.7°C, was taken at Al-Aziziyah, south of Tripoli, Libya. In coastal regions the high temperatures are accompanied by high atmospheric humidity, producing uncomfortable climatic conditions. Away from the coasts the generally clear skies produce a large diurnal range and frost is not uncommon in many places during the night. The eastern Sahara is the sunniest area in the world, with a 97% average.

Map 4 Winds and Rainfall

High pressure is the dominant feature of the Arab lands. This is due to descending air currents in the Horse latitudes. Winds are generally light, though strong sand winds are sporadic, unpleasant occurrences which can persist for days. Rainfall is generally low and the rate of surface evaporation high, leading to arid conditions over much of the area. The aridity is intensified by the irregular nature of the rainfall. Heavy showers may be followed by months, or in extreme cases even years, without appreciable precipitation. The Mediterranean littoral has a higher rainfall, largely on account of depressions that originate in the Atlantic and cross the Mediterranean in the winter months.

Map 5 Natural Vegetation

Most of the area has little more than scanty shrub vegetation. Only in parts of the extreme north and south are there appreciable amounts of grass. Although swamp grass is the natural vegetation of the lower valleys of the Nile, Tigris and Euphrates, much of it has now vanished as a result of agricultural development.

Map 6 Population

It should be borne in mind that the populations and densities are computed on a national basis, disregarding regional considerations. For example, virtually the whole of Egypt's considerable population is concentrated in the valley and delta of the Nile and the greater part of the country is uninhabited.

A hidden factor in the map of average annual population growth rate is the influx of foreigners into the oil-rich Gulf states. By the same token, the figures for Lebanon have been affected in the other direction by the hostilities in the area. Map source: UN Demographic Yearbook 1978.

Map 7 Health and Medical Care

The pattern of health and medical care in the Arab countries reflects the division of rich and poor. The oil exporting countries of North Africa and the Gulf generally speaking have the highest number of hospital beds. In the diagram infant mortality is taken as the number of deaths of children under one year per 1,000 live births, and should be compared with a world average of just under 100. Life expectancy, which is the average number of years a child can expect to live, does not always equate to the current availability of medical services. In the light of known development plans for health care the 1980s will see a widening of the gap between rich and poor Arab countries. Saudi Arabia, Kuwait, the UAE and Qatar plan to spend billions of dollars on hospitals and community health care making use of private health care companies from Europe and the United States.

Because of a welfare state philosophy urgent health problems can be treated at government expense in the West where facilities at home are lacking. By contrast countries such as Mauritania, North Yemen, South Yemen and Somalia have some of the worst social indicators in the world with few resources available. Map source: UN Demographic Yearbook 1978.

Map 8 Food and Nutrition

Self sufficiency in food production is the aim of most Arab countries. The Gulf states have long had a dream of investing petrodollars in the large agricultural countries of the Arab world such as Egypt and Sudan to grow the food they need. Instead it has proved easier to buy frozen food and commodities from Europe, the US, South America and Australasia. The hungry in the Arab world are to be found in the poorest countries — Mauritania, Somalia and the two Yemens. The well fed live in the Gulf states or in countries with viable agriculture such as Sudan and Egypt. Before oil was exported from the Gulf in large quantities the diet of gulf nationals was composed largely of dates, rice, camel milk and fish. Meat was an occasional dish usually consumed on feast days only. The culinary tradition owed more to the Indian sub-continent than to Arab countries such as Lebanon or Syria. Today the people of the Gulf states eat a diet which is influenced by the West and includes more meat than ever before. Mutton and lamb are preferred choices but chicken meat consumption has risen rapidly. Frozen foods and modern vacuum packaging has made it easy for Gulf states to import high quality products from the West. Halal slaughter to comply with religious precepts has been introduced in many of the producing countries which must also now comply with strict date stamping, Arabic food labelling and entry requirements. Map source: State of Food and Agriculture (FAO 1980).

Map 9 Literacy and Learning

Egypt and Lebanon have been the traditional centres of Arabic learning and culture. Kuwait because of its large Palestinian population also has a highly educated population. Egyptian and Jordanian teachers, recruited to work in the Gulf states, are striving to raise standards both of education and adult literacy. Universities have been established in all the Gulf states except Oman where the country's first — Qaboos University — is under construction. The criterion of literacy used in the diagram is the ability to both read and write. World figures for comparison are a literacy rate of just over 70 per cent and an expenditure on education of nearly 6 per cent of GNP. The highest spending on education in the 1980s will be by the oil rich Gulf states where the majority of the population is under 21. Under government programmes students from the Gulf states move on to further education in Europe and the US. When the lower Gulf states achieved independence in the 1970s there were fewer than 1,000 graduates. Today the emphasis is on building national cadres to reduce the dependence on expatriate labour. Students from the poorer Arab countries are able to attend universities and colleges in the Gulf under inter-Arab co-operation programmes. Map source: UNESCO Statistical Yearbook 1981.

Map 10 Standard of Living

The oil surplus states of Saudi Arabia, Kuwait, the UAE and Qatar have the highest per capita incomes in the world. In general wealth has been dispersed throughout their societies because of the small and manageable size of their populations. At the other end of the scale the two Yemens, Somalia, Sudan and Mauritania rank among the poorest countries of the world although the figures often fail to tell the full story. More than 1 million Yemenis are thought to work in the Gulf states sending home valuable remittances which fail to show through in official figures. Through generous aid programmes — sometimes amounting to more than 5 per cent of GNP — the surplus states have given no strings attached aid to other Arab and Islamic countries. Despite these aid programmes the differences between rich and poor in the Arab world are likely to increase. Saudi Arabia has since 1978 installed more than 1 million telephone lines. Nomadic tribesmen who 10 years ago drove camels now have shiny Mercedes trucks assembled in the kingdom. Air travel which was a rarity in the 1950s is now commonplace with the Arab world linked by excellent communications. For the poorer countries multilateral aid, bank borrowing and technical assistance programmes offer the best hope of raising the standard of living. Map source: World Bank 1981.

Map 11 Standards Compared

The per capita GNP of Arab countries is slightly lower than the world average of $2,400 despite the fact that the oil surplus states rank among the richest in the world. This reflects the small population of the richest Arab countries — more than 50 per cent of whose populations are expatriate — compared to the large populations of high absorbing countries such as Egypt, Sudan and Algeria. With the oil surplus of OPEC dwindling to less than $9,000 million in 1982 there is likely to be a pause in the relative rise of living standards of Arab countries compared with the rest of the world. Saudi Arabia, the UAE, Qatar and Kuwait will have less money to spend on development at home and aid abroad although vital current expenditure will be maintained at the level of the early 1980s. The need to spend huge sums of money on defence because of big power ambitions in the Arabian Gulf will further divert funds from social infrastructure. In Oman it is estimated that 40 per cent of national income goes on maintaining the defence forces in a state of readiness. Every government in the Arab region is anxious to stimulate private sector initiatives although in some there is a socialist system of government. Only South Yemen is an openly Marxist state. Map source: World Bank 1981 (GNP per capita); UN Statistical Yearbook 1978 (telephones and cars).

Map 12 Employment

Jobs for nationals is a goal of the states of the Arabian Gulf which continue to import expatriate labour from other Arab countries, the Indian sub-continent and Europe. The numbers of expatriates have not become as overwhelming as in Nigeria where expulsions have taken place. Many Gulf states are nevertheless concerned about the number of 'foreigners' in their midst fearing that their Arab and Islamic culture will be 'swamped'. A major constraint on the greater employment of nationals in some Arab countries, notably Saudi Arabia and Qatar, are the restrictions on women. Women can only work in reserved occupations in Saudi Arabia including teaching and medicine. Other Gulf states which adhere to less strict interpretations of Islam allow women to work in office jobs and retailing. The economically active population has been taken as the total of employed people and unemployed people but excludes students, the retired and social dependents. Agriculture in many countries is still the largest employer despite the urban tradition developing, particularly in the Gulf states, of people dwelling together in air conditioned city blocks. A drift from the land has nevertheless taken place in the Gulf with many villages being abandoned as the inhabitants left for the cities. In some cases nomadic Bedu have been forcibly re-settled. Map sources: State of Food and Agriculture (FAO 1980); World Statistics in Brief (UN 1981).

Map 13 Land Use

The countries of the Arab world are dominated in their use of land by the high proportion of uncultivatable desert. As the map shows, huge tracts of land serve little or no economic activity. The richest areas, from the agricultural point of view, are the north African littoral and the Nile delta, and in the eastern Mediterranean, Lebanon and Syria. The resourcefulness and determination of the people to support their way of life in very adverse conditions is shown by the wide incidence of nomadic herding. Such nomad tribesmen who have mastered the desert for thousands of years continue in many regions to lead their same hardy life today.

The determining factor in land use is water supplies, hence the overwhelming importance of water resources in the Arab world. With new technology and techniques of desalination, there is a good prospect for much better use of land in the Arab world in the years to come, with a corresponding benefit in the ability of countries to feed their populations. Map source: FAO Production Yearbook 1980; Statistical abstracts for individual countries.

Map 14 Agriculture

The aim of making the desert bloom has become a

reality for the rich Gulf states which have lavished development funds on their semi-arid land. Expenditure is sometimes out of proportion to the strict economics of a project but often farming is undertaken for strategic or prestige reasons. In countries such as Qatar farming is a rich man's hobby rather than a practical way of feeding even a small population of less than 250,000. Rather than spend their money on 'greening' the desert, Gulf states have been urged to invest in agriculture in Egypt and the Sudan. Political misunderstandings and the practicalities of managing such investments have frustrated many attempts to turn these African countries into the 'bread basket of the Arab world'. Better road communications have improved the potential for export of fresh produce from countries such as Lebanon and Jordan to the Gulf. The best example of a pan Arab agricultural project which has fulfilled some of the ideals so often expounded is the Kenana sugar project in Sudan where Kuwaiti investment and western management have combined with Sudanese labour to create a viable sugar export industry. The project was, however, delayed some years by poor communications within the Sudan and differences between the parties concerned. Map sources: FAO Production Yearbook 1980; statistical abstracts for individual countries.

Map 15 Livestock

A preference for lamb and mutton in the diets of most Arabs is reflected in the make up of the national herds. The Gulf states and the Arabian peninsula countries in general are net importers of meat. Live sheep are shipped from Australia to the Red Sea and the Gulf in quantities approaching 6 million head a year. Of late chicken meat imports have slightly reduced the demand for lamb and mutton but this remains high. Due to the war with Iran the Iraqi herd is believed to be almost decimated. The predominant livestock animal is, apart from the question of taste and diet, a reflection of the nature of pasture. The map should be compared with Map 5 (vegetation) for a full picture. Goats thrive in a semi-urban environment because of their appetite for roughage which can be satisfied by urban waste and even rubbish. This makes goats particularly suited to the Gulf states. Outbreaks of foot and mouth disease have in recent years frustrated the attempts of the Gulf states to improve their national herds. It has become common to see prize cattle in air-conditioned pens in quite distant parts of Saudi Arabia but in general cattle are reared in the Gulf states less for their meat than for the dairy produce which is an important constituent of diets there. The camel is prized by the Bedouin as a beast of burden but also for its sweet milk and meat. Map source: FAO Production Yearbook 1980.

Map 16 The Balance of Farming

The oil producing states of the Gulf, together with Libya, are the biggest importers of food. In countries such as Oman it is estimated that as much as 20 per cent of food production is wasted because of poor distribution and marketing. Farmers can, however, show unusual initiative where the returns are high. In North Yemen much valuable farmland which once grew wheat and coffee has been turned over to plantations of a narcotic leaf called qat which is chewed daily by the male population. Egypt, despite its ability to produce food, is nevertheless one of the world's biggest importers of grain after the Soviet Union. In the Gulf states Iraq, because of the war with Iran, has stepped up the pace of its food imports. Saudi Arabia has a smaller population but spends proportionately more on food imports. Meat and luxury foods make up the largest proportion of the imports of food by the rich Gulf states but nearly all supply nationals of their countries with subsidised essentials — rice, sugar and flour. Changing tastes have created huge demand for canned soft drinks, fast foods and packaged products of all kinds. Map sources: UN Statistical Yearbook 1978; statistical abstracts of individual countries; World Statistics in Brief (UN 1981).

Map 17 Mineral Wealth

Gold has been discovered in Saudi Arabia at a site which some believe was the fabled King Solomon's mines. Although hardly sufficient to challenge South Africa the discovery points to the likelihood of other minerals under the Arabian peninsula soil. Oman is thought to have some of the oldest rocks in the world and in 1983 exports of refined copper ore will start — the first non hydrocarbons mineral export by the peninsula countries. It is often stated, however, that the Arab world has little in the way of mineral wealth apart from oil and gas. Large deposits of phosphates exist in Morocco and Libya has searched for uranium ore. Cement production is possible in most Arab countries using natural raw materials. Some minerals processing industries have been established in the Gulf using imported raw materials. Bahrain and Dubai both have aluminium smelters, even though the alumina is imported from Australia and Brazil. This is because resources of cheap gas can be used to produce the aluminium at lower prices than elsewhere provided the world market price for aluminium remains high. Exploration for minerals is taking place in many Arab countries with a particularly exhaustive search being undertaken by Saudi Arabia and Sudan under the Red Sea.

Map 18 Oil Production

Saudi Arabia is in normal times the world's biggest exporter of oil outside the Soviet bloc. Weak market prices for oil and a mild winter in Europe had in early 1983 resulted in oil production cuts by Saudi Arabia and its Gulf allies of Qatar, Kuwait and the UAE. A land-slide away from the OPEC benchmark price of $34 a barrel was possible with some pessimists forecasting an oil price of less than $20 a barrel by late 1983. The increase of oil production in the Arab world between 1970-80 was 39 per cent compared with 26 per cent for the rest of the world. In 1979

particularly high levels of production were achieved. Actual oil output by the Arab countries usually follows OPEC decisions on production but some countries which export oil are not OPEC members — notably Egypt, Oman, Bahrain and Syria. Within the UAE, Dubai, which sells 360,000 barrels a day, does not observe OPEC policies since it retains autonomy over oil policy. Iraq's ability to export its oil has been severely limited by its war with Iran. In April 1982 Syria closed the overland pipeline Iraq was using to the Mediterranean. Production levels given on the map reflect theoretical capacity rather than actual production at least where the larger producers are concerned. Saudi production, for example, in early 1983 was less than 5 million barrels a day (b/d) close to the minimum required by the government to maintain expenditure targets. Map source: BP Statistical Review of the World Oil Industry (1980).

Map 19 The Movement of Oil

The oil price rises of the 1970s brought about a greater awareness in western countries of the need to reduce energy consumption. At the same time non-OPEC sources of oil have become more important. By late 1982 non OPEC countries were selling 20 million barrels a day of oil against 18 million b/d by OPEC countries. The biggest users of Arab oil and gas remain the Europeans, Americans and the Japanese. No Saudi oil is sold to the Soviet bloc for political reasons. An era of cheaper oil which seemed likely in early 1983 would probably stimulate more exports of oil from Arab countries to newly industrialised countries such as South Korea and Brazil. Indonesia, Malaysia and other Asian countries would be likely purchasers. In the map oil production and inter-regional oil movements are based on 1980 figures and oil reserves are as at 1 January 1981. In 1980 Arab oil production accounted for a third of the world total and exports for almost two-thirds of the world total. The proven reserves were over half the world total ensuring that Arab countries will continue to play a pivotal role in the world energy equation until well into the next century. Map sources: Oil and Gas Journal; B.P. Statistical Review of the World Oil Industry (1980).

Map 20 Energy Consumption

Energy consumption is rising rapidly in the rich Gulf states where rising standards of living have created huge demand for air conditioning and other comforts. The drive to create downstream industries for the day when the oil runs dry has also increased the need for power generation. Lack of natural water resources has accelerated the demand for more water to be produced by desalination. By 1990 many of the rich Gulf states will be examining nuclear options for power stations and desalination plant. In the map the energy data is based on consumption of many different fuels but is represented in coal equivalent. Coal is, however, a fuel little used in Arab countries. The average world per capita energy consumption is just over 2,000 kilogrammes of coal equivalent. The big spenders in the Arab world on energy projects are Saudi Arabia, Iraq, the UAE, Kuwait, Libya and Egypt. The possibility of a national grid for the Arabian peninsula countries has been examined within the context of the Gulf co-operation Council (GCC), a regional grouping established in 1981, but due to the incompatibility of present systems this seems unlikely. Countries currently carrying out electricity projects worth separately in excess of $1,000 million include Kuwait at Al Zour, Abu Dhabi at Taweelah and Saudi Arabia in the Eastern Province. Map sources: World Statistics in Brief (UN 1979); yearbook of World Energy Statistics (UN 1981).

Map 21 Industry and Manufacturing

Industrial cities have been created from the sand on the shores of the Gulf and the Red Sea in recent years. The oil producing states including the North African countries all wish to put oil revenue to use in diversifying the base of their economies in preparation for the time when they cease to be exporters of hydrocarbons. Industrial development has been less dramatic in non-oil producing countries such as Lebanon and Jordan despite the existence of a trained and skilled workforce. Many skilled workers from countries of the Near East have left for better paid jobs in the Gulf. The industries with the best hope of success in Arab countries are, however, those linked to oil production. Refining, gas liquefaction, fertilisers and petrochemicals all draw on the existence of cheap energy and fuelstock. They remain vulnerable, nevertheless, to weakness in the markets of the developed countries where overstocking of gas and petrochemicals has occurred. Because cheap fuel is often dependent on high levels of oil production, since the industrial cities use gas which is produced with crude oil as a by-product, industrial output is not always constant. In addition the Gulf has experienced problems with developing new industries because of the harshness of the environment and the corrosion in the atmosphere. Map sources: UN Statistical Yearbook (1978); Statistical abstracts of individual countries; Middle East and North Africa 1981-82 (Europa Publications).

Map 22 Volume of Trade

Crude oil and processed gas sales represent more than 90 per cent of Gross Domestic Product (GDP) in the richest Arab countries. Wealth from oil gives Saudi Arabia, the Gulf states of Kuwait, Qatar and the UAE, a huge trade surplus despite their dependence on industrialised countries for capital goods and commodities. Until recently the Gulf was not even self sufficient in refined products — having to import the petrol to power the motor vehicles which took the oilmen to the oil fields. In non oil producing countries such as Sudan, Mauritania, North Yemen and Somalia the value of imports, often ironically largely of hydrocarbons, exceeds that of exports, in some cases by a factor of four or more. The volume of trade

between Arab countries has traditionally been small but is increasing. The Iraq-Iran war has led to more transhipment trade between the Gulf ports and through Aqaba in Jordan. Better roads in the Arabian peninsula have stimulated inter-Arab trade. It is now possible to drive on asphalted road from Amman in Jordan to Salalah in southern Oman. Through the Abu Dhabi based Arab Monetary Fund (AMF) a technical scheme has been evolved to allow Arab countries to trade in Arab Units of Account. Should trade between Arab countries increase to a significant volume it is possible that more integration at this level would take place. Map sources: Direction of World Trade (IMF 1981); Statistical abstracts of individual countries.

Map 23 Trading Partners

The trading partners of the Arab countries are naturally enough the world's biggest trading nations: Japan, the United States, West Germany, France, Italy, the United Kingdom and other members of the European Economic Community (EEC). A realisation of the enormous volumes of hydrocarbons being bought from Arab states in the 1970s spurred most industrialised countries to mount a trade drive in the Arabian peninsula and the rich North African countries. Other newly industrialised countries including South Korea, whose construction companies dominate the rich contracting market, have been quick to see the potential for sales to the Arab world. Japan leads largely because of her exports of motor vehicles but also because of supplies of telecommunications equipment and consumer goods. Because of hydrocarbons exports the Arab countries as a whole are a net exporter. In 1980 exports totalled just over $200,000 million and imports at just over $100,000 million of which Saudi Arabia probably represented more than 30 per cent. With Iraq locked in combat with Iran, Saudi Arabia is once again the biggest Arab market — to the UK it is worth more than all British trade with the Soviet Union and eastern Europe added together and the same level of importance attaches to most industrialised countries. Map source: Direction of World Trade (IMF 1981).

Map 24 National Wealth

The wealth of Arab countries is based on oil, with Saudi Arabia far and away the most important producer, both absolutely and in relation to its population. But this over-reliance on a single commodity has caused Arab nations fundamental problems in their economic development. At time of economic expansion, demand for oil is high and prices firm; but at times of international recession, countries so dependent on a single commodity face major dislocation of their economic development plans. Moreover, while the income from oil has risen dramatically in the good years, growing strains on the international monetary system, with Arab countries inextricably dependent on the United States dollar, have raised new problems.

Saudi Arabia has taken a firm lead in assisting less fortunate Arab countries which have small or only limited oil production, and has also played a key role in international efforts to 'recycle' petro-dollars. The most populous member of the Arab world, Egypt, which has made strenuous efforts to build a modern manufacturing economy, has lately joined the ranks of oil producers too. Map sources: International Financial Statistics (IMF 1980); The World in Facts and Figures (The Economist).

Map 25 Wealth of the Arab World

The Arab world has always been rich in culture and tradition. Since the three fold rise in oil prices of 1973, followed by the second round of oil price rises of 1979, large surpluses have been accumulated by Saudi Arabia, Kuwait, the UAE and Qatar. Other Arab oil producers including Egypt and Oman also have a healthier balance of payments because of oil sales. By comparison with the developing world, where most of the Arab oil surpluses are invested, the resources of the Arab world are slight. They compare favourably with other areas of the developing world particularly black Africa. The institutions in the Arab world which manage the surplus have tended to be conservative investors preferring blue chip investments in US Treasury stocks and West German bonds and securities. Of late Arab money has been invested in public companies including some of the industrial giants of the western world. In the 1980s Arab investors will be more prepared to enter risk ventures and will seek a role in management. The map compares the total GNP of the Arab countries with that of other regions of the world. The GNP figures for Europe include the eastern bloc countries, but the international reserves for these countries are not available. The figure for the international reserves of the Soviet Union is also unavailable. Map sources: UN Monthly Bulletin of Statistics, February 1982; International Financial Statistics (IMF 1981).

Map 26 Development of the Arab World

Development in the Arab world has been most rapid in the oil producing states of the Arabian Gulf. The map fails to give data for the Lower Gulf states since reporting by these countries before independence in the early 1970s was uneven. Some countries have achieved impressive annual growth in GNP but starting from a very low level. North Yemen, for example, has some of the worst social indicators in the world despite having an average annual increase in GNP of more than 10 per cent a year. Fairly low average increases in the native population of the Gulf states have occured since 1960 due to rising standards of living and wider practice of birth control which is not forbidden by Islam. By contrast the poorest countries have become increasingly dependent on Arab and multilateral aid. Wars and famine within the Arab world have tended to retard development in some countries — notably Iraq where the costs of reconstruction after the war with Iran are already estimated at more than $50,000

million, Lebanon which was ravaged by civil war and an Israeli invasion in 1982 and Somalia which has suffered from war with its neighbour Ethiopia and the affects of famine and locusts. Egypt has made a reasonable recovery from the 1973 war with Israel but this owes much to its status as an oil producer. Map source: World Development Handbook.

Map 27 By Road and Rail

Road improvements particularly in the Arabian peninsula have been a major factor in boosting the economy of the Arab nation. Trucks carrying vegetables from Jordan and Lebanon can reach Salalah in South Oman within 10 days. Oil wealth has meant that the traditional barriers to surface communications — the Sahara and Arabian desert — have been overcome. Land transport from Europe to the Gulf states was first popular in the mid-1970s when severe congestion existed at Gulf and Red Sea ports. With the closure of some Iraqi ports because of the war with Iran it has once again come into its own. Although the population density of some Arab countries in the Gulf would not warrant an ambitious network of roads sufficient wealth exists to make this feasible. Infrastructure has been put in place by the Gulf states with the future in mind rather than present needs. Railway projects in Iraq and Saudi Arabia are receiving attention from the governments concerned. High speed trains travelling at more than 250 kilometres an hour are to be purchased by Iraq. Saudi Arabia's only operating railway is between Riyadh, the capital, and the Dammam-Al-Khobar-Dhahran complex which is the oil producing area. Plans exist to reinstate the ancient Hejaz railway which once connected Damascus and the pilgrim city of Medina. A British subsidiary of the state railway organisation British Rail is also working on a feasibility plan for a Gulf railway connecting the Iraqi rail system with Kuwait, Saudi Arabia, the UAE and Oman. Map sources: Middle East and North Africa 1981-82 (Europa Publications); International Road Federation; International Union of Railways.

Map 28 By Sea and Air

A huge increase in port and airport capacity in the oil producing countries took place in the 1970s. To a lesser extent port improvements, using grant aid, took place in the poorer Arab states as a result of improved communications in general. North Yemen, for example, was able to bring its port of Hedeidah up to modern standards and has an international airport at Sanaa capable of handling the biggest jet aircraft. By the end of the 1970s it was apparent that too many berths and airports had been built in some countries. The United Arab Emirates (UAE) has four fully operational international airports with two more planned. In one case — Dubai and Sharjah — the runways almost touch. Dubai also has a 74-berth industrial port — as big as Rotterdam — but it is running at very low occupancy. Gulf ports have however increased their business because of the Iran-Iraq war since it is now necessary to tranship goods to smaller vessels or land transport for on shipment to Iraq. To a much lesser extent Dubai is carrying on some transhipment trade with Iran. Saudi Arabia's decision to build a pipeline from the eastern oil fields to the Red Sea at Yanbu has resulted in more tanker traffic using the Suez Canal. Petroleum exports are a major factor in the total tonnage handled by the principal ports of the Arab world. Air freight has been used increasingly as a method for shipping in perishable goods such as chilled meat as well as vital spares and parts for the oil fields and industrial complexes. The Gulf would in any case, even without oil, be an important stopping point for passenger aircraft flying between London and the Far East since it is mid-way between Singapore and London and Hong Kong and London. Map sources: UN Statistical Yearbook 1978; Statistical abstracts of individual countries; Middle East and North Africa 1981-82 (Europa Publications).

Map 29 The Media

Egypt and Lebanon were the traditional centres of the Middle East press. The Cairo daily Al-Ahram under its editor Mohammad Heikal could justifiably consider itself the leading newspaper of the Arab world. After the bilateral peace between Egypt and Israel reached following the Camp David accords the Egyptian media became less important because of the ostracising of Egypt from the Arab fold. Censorship in Arab countries, a product of the state of war existing between the hardline states and Israel, has presented difficulties for many publishers. Some have used this, and the disorders in Beirut, as a reason to locate offshore in Cyprus or London. The leading London Arabic daily As Sharq al-Awsat, which is Saudi owned, could now possibly claim to have taken over the mantle of press leadership once held by Al-Ahram. The Gulf states have invested large sums of money in television and radio stations buying 'state of the art' technology in many cases. The radio transmitters are used to spread truth about Islam and also to present the Arab view of the Palestinian question. Television is seen as a way of preserving Arab culture although initially its use was resisted by conservative clerics. The Arabic press co-exists with a thriving English language press in the Gulf states. Business magazines have been particularly successful as a medium for advertising, but in English, since the language of business in the Gulf tends to be English rather than Arabic. Map sources: World Statistics in Brief (UN 1981); UNESCO Statistical Yearbook.

Map 30 Government and Politics

Arabs believe that there is one Arab nation and reluctantly accept that there are 21 Arab countries — including what they call Palestine. The latter is not recognised as a state since it is subjugated by Israel. There have been many attempts at confederation and unity (ittihad) between Arab countries. Only one federation — the United Arab Emirates (UAE), a union of seven sheikhdoms founded in 1971, is in existence today. Libya and Egypt have been two countries which have tried many times to federate but political differences have forced them apart. The oldest organisation dedicated to Arab unity is the Arab League but the Arab world's biggest country — Egypt — has been excluded because of its peace treaty with Israel. In the Gulf the newest attempt at unity is the Gulf Co-operation Council — modelled on the EEC but broadened to include defence and security. This is a grouping, founded in 1981, of Kuwait, Saudi Arabia, Bahrain, Oman the UAE and Qatar. Iraq is not a member but the possibility of enlargement to include the Yemens and Jordan has been hinted at. On the economic front Arab oil producers have formed the Organisation of Arab Petroleum Exporting Countries (OAPEC), based in Kuwait. This is not important as a price fixing cartel but has sponsored a number of downstream projects including a Bahrain dry dock. Among the most recent attempts at political unity have been Egypt and Sudan (an accord was signed in 1982) and the two Yemens (talks about a constitutional union continue to take place). Iraq and Syria which were close to unity a few years ago have since quarrelled bitterly. Syria subsequently blocked the Iraqi oil pipeline to the Mediterranean in April 1982 and has backed Iran in the Gulf war. Other inter Arab disputes exist between Algeria and Morocco over the status of the former Spanish Sahara and between several of the Gulf emirates over boundary demarcations.

Map 31 Military Expenditure

Arab armies have been built up through successive wars with Israel over the Palestine question. The hardline Arab states confronting Israel — Syria, Jordan and Iraq, have continued to build up their forces since the inconclusive 1973 war. Egypt has maintained a high level of military spending despite its bilateral peace with Israel. Backed by the United States Egypt remains the backbone of the Arab army. The big spenders on military hardware in the 1980s will be the Gulf states. Only Oman has a direct military threat to its security. South Yemen has been a consistent supporter since the early 1970s of rebels opposed to Sultan Qaboos. The oil producing Gulf states are building up their defences through concern over the Soviet invasion of Afghanistan and because of the vulnerability of the oil fields to attack or sabotage. In building their arsenals they can afford the most advanced equipment available including F-16 and Mirage interceptors and sophisticated electronic command systems. Iraq's war with Iran is costing that country an estimated $1,000 million a month. Bankrolled by the Arab Gulf states Iraq is keeping the revolutionary armies at bay. The Soviet Union is present in South Yemen with military bases which the United States has sought to counter by agreeing a military access treaty with Oman. This would mean that US troops could take up stations in the Gulf should a general emergency occur. Map sources: The Military Balance 1981-82 (Institute for Strategical Studies); World Bank; World Military Expenditure and Arms transfer 1969-78 (USACDA).

Map 32 Military Might

The frontline states confronting Israel — Syria, Jordan and Iraq — have the largest collective armed forces. Egypt, which in 1979 agreed a bilateral peace with Israel, has maintained its large standing army despite the peace policies of Presidents Sadat and Mubarak. Libya which has threatened war with Egypt and claims sovereignty over the Bay of Sirte has considerable military strength as has Algeria which has differences with Morocco over the status of the former Spanish Sahara. The Omanis have the best trained forces among the Gulf states, despite their small size of some 17,000 men, with Jaguar interceptors and missile carrying patrol boats supplied by Britain. Saudi Arabia has the biggest military budget in the Gulf (apart from Iraq) and is purchasing advanced equipment from the United States. The Gulf states have been obliged to rely on mercenaries from other Arab countries and Pakistan to man their armies. Technical advisers and some senior posts have been filled by Europeans and Americans. The US Army Corps of Engineers is playing an important role in developing the Saudi defence programme and a similar role is played by the U.K. in Oman. Moroccans, Pakistanis and Jordanians are the most frequent nationalities to serve as enlisted men and non commissioned officers in Gulf armies. In North Yemen the defence forces are being trained by both Soviet and US advisers — a unique situation in the Arab world. The Soviet Union maintains a base on the island of Socotra in the Indian Ocean which belongs to South Yemen. Map sources: The Military Balance 1981-82 (Institute for Stratregical Studies); World Military Expenditure and Arms Transfer 1969-78 (USACDA).

Map 33 Comparative Military Strength

The Arab defence forces are collectively small when compared to other regional groupings. The percentage of GNP spent on defence is, however, high reflecting the state of military readiness which Arab countries have maintained since the formation of the present state of Israel. Whatever the outcome of the present round of fighting between Iran and Iraq, most observers believe that the trend will be for the Arab countries to increase their military spending and to continue to amass armaments and military strength. At present no Arab country possesses nuclear knowhow but attempts have been made by a friendly state — Pakistan — to secure this knowledge. The balance of friendship in the Arab world has switched in the past 10 years to a much more pro-western line although it is possible that the next generation of leaders, in the Gulf states in particular, will wish to adopt a more non-aligned posture. Of Arab states only Syria and South Yemen have open and large programmes of co-operation in military matters with the Soviet Union. South Yemen is in fact a member of the Comecon trading bloc. Map sources: The Military Balance 1981-82 (Institute for Stratregical Studies); World Military Expenditure and Arms transfer 1969-78 (USACDA).

Map 34 The Cradles of Civilization

The areas now occupied by the Arab nations contain two of the earliest cradles of civilization — the valleys of the Nile and the Tigris/Euphrates. The main map shows the core regions of civilization c. 1500 BC. The maximum extent of the early empires at various times is shown on the small maps. Assyrian inscriptions of the 9th century BC refer to Arab nomads inhabiting the northern part of the Arabian peninsula.

Map 35 The Classical Influence

The Roman empire is shown at its greatest overall extent in AD 116. The Persian empire is shown at its greatest extent under the Sasanian king Shapur I, following the defeat and capture of the Roman emperor Valerian. At this time the Arab peoples were confined to the Arabian peninsula and the desert areas of the Middle East.

Map 36 The Expansion of Islam

Between Mohammed's forced withdrawal to Medina in 622 and his death in 632 the Islamic religion gained sway over most of Arabia. The further advance of the Arab conquerors and their new religion was facilitated by the disintegration of the Roman and Persian empires. At its height the Arab empire stretched from the Atlantic Ocean in the west to central Asia in the east. Today Islam has spread far beyond the Arab conquests. The most populous Muslim countries are in fact Indonesia and Bangladesh.

Map 37 The Arab World in Eclipse

By 1600 the Ottomans held sway over most of the Arab lands and continued to do so for the next two centuries. The decline of the Ottoman empire during the 19th century, and the reduction of its power in many areas to nominal control, paved the way for its complete disintegration following world War 1. By 1939 only two countries — Saudi Arabia and Yemen — were totally outside the control of European Powers.

Map 38 National Resurgence

There was a great resurgence of confidence in the Arab world during the 1970s, despite all the many problems of individual states and, in many cases, bitter national rivalries. The reason for the rebirth of pan-Arab morale was in large measure a consequence of the Opec cartel, which showed that the oil producers could effectively wield their authority in the modern world. While the decline of Opec as a price cartel in the early 1980s will reduce this influence from an economic standpoint, many of the political gains achieved are likely to remain, such as improved relations with the United States and the European Community.

In most cases Arab independence was achieved

in the years after World War II, The dates given against the flags are when independence was declared. The colour background in the map indicates the period when total independence was realized. In some cases, notably where special treaty relations existed, dates vary considerably.

ACKNOWLEDGEMENTS

Algeria, Libya, People's Democratic Republic of Yemen: Zefa; Bahrain: Steve Kibble; Djibouti, Mauritania, Western Sahara, Saudi Arabia: Robert Harding Associates; Egypt, Jordan, Syria: Sonia Halliday; Iraq: Iraqi Cultural Centre; Kuwait: David Butler; Lebanon: Lebanon Tourist Office; Morocco: Ken Merryless; Oman: Shell Photo Service; Qatar: Qatar Embassy; Sudan: Helene Rogers; Tunisia: Tunisia Tourist Office; Dubai: David Butler; Yemen Arab Republic: William Reeve.